MW01014995

An Introduction to
Assembly Language
Programming
for the 8086 Family

More than three million people have learned to program, use and enjoy microcomputers with Wiley Press Guides. Look for these titles and others at your local book or computer store.

Other Computer Titles from Wiley Press

An Introduction to Assembly Language Programming for the 8086 Family, Skinner
Expert Systems: Artificial Intelligence in Business, Harmon & King
Introduction to 8080/8085 Assembly Language, Fernandez & Ashley
6502 Assembly Language Programming, Fernandez/Tabler/Ashley
8080/Z80 Assembly Language Programming, Miller
The 8087 Primer, Palmer & Morse
*80286 Architecture, Morse & Albert

*Forthcoming title

Wiley Press books are available at quantity discounts when used to promote products or services. For information, please write to the Special Sales Department, John Wiley & Sons.

An Introduction to Assembly Language Programming for the 8086 Family

A Self-Teaching Guide

THOMAS P. SKINNER, Ph.D.
Boston University

A Wiley Press Book
JOHN WILEY & SONS, INC.
New York • Chichester • Brisbane • Toronto • Singapore

Publisher: Stephen Kippur
Editor: Theron Shreve
Managing Editor: Katherine Schowalter
Composition & Design: Ganis & Harris, Inc.

Intel® is a registered trademark of Intel Corporation.

Copyright © 1985 by John Wiley & Sons, Inc.

All rights reserved. Published simultaneously in Canada.

Reproduction or translation of any part of this work beyond
that permitted by Section 107 or 108 of the 1976 United States
Copyright Act without the permission of the copyright owner
is unlawful. Requests for permission or further information
should be addressed to the Permissions Department, John
Wiley & Sons, Inc.

Library of Congress Cataloging in Publication Data

Skinner, Thomas P.
    An introduction to assembly language programming
for the 8086 family.

    Includes index.
    1. Assembler language (Computer program language)
2. Intel 8086 (Microprocessor)—Programming.
3. Intel 8088 (Microprocessor)—Programming.   I. Title.
QA76.73.A8S57   1985   001.64′24   85-9409
ISBN 0-471-80825-3

Printed in the United States of America

85 86 10 9 8 7 6 5 4 3 2 1

In memory of my mother

ACKNOWLEDGMENTS

I would like to thank the numerous individuals who provided support and encouragement. My wife, Linda, deserves special thanks. The Intel Corporation and Digital Research were generous in providing me with substantial documentation.

PREFACE

Is this book for you? If you have essentially no familiarity with computers, especially microcomputers, this is not the book for you. You should obtain one of the many introductory level books that delve into computer basics. If you do have some familiarity with computer use, such as having used a word processor or spreadsheet, but have never learned to program, this may still not be the book for you. It is preferable to first learn a high-level programming language such as BASIC or PASCAL before trying to learn assembly language.

This book is aimed at readers who have had some programming experience in a high-level language and may know an assembly language for some other computer. Readers with an assembly language background will find this book an easy way to learn the 8086/8088. But if you don't know a bit from a register, don't worry; it will be explained. You should, however, know what a file is, have some understanding of operating systems like CP/M, PC-DOS, or MS-DOS, and understand the basics of writing a program.

HOW TO USE THIS BOOK

This Self-Teaching Guide consists of 15 chapters. Read the chapters in the order presented. Each chapter builds on the material introduced in the previous chapter. Chapter 1 covers number systems. It is essential that you know about binary and hexadecimal numbers and arithmetic before we can talk about assembly language. If you already have this background, you might skim this chapter. Chapter 2 introduces the 8086/8088 family architecture. Chapter 3 discusses the format of an assembly language program. This format is what you will use when entering the source program, using your editor. Chapter 4 is where you actually get going. By the end of Chapter 4, you will be able to write and execute a complete program. The faster you get going in actually writing and running programs, the easier it will be to learn the material. That is why I attempt to get you off the ground as quickly as possible.

Chapters 5 through 13 cover the complete instruction set of the 8086/8088 in a sequence that keeps building. You will be able to write progressively more sophisticated programs. These chapters also include additional material on assembler features that you will need to know.

Chapter 14 talks about the special hardware features of the 80186 and 80188 microprocessors. In addition to special hardware features, these microprocessors have additional instructions that the 8086 and 8088 do not have. Chapter 15 introduces the very powerful 80286.

Included with each chapter are questions and answers designed to test your mastery of the key points. Please take the time to answer these questions and to check your results. Once again, let me emphasize that the best way to learn a programming language is to actually write and run programs. Don't wait until you have read the entire book. Start as soon as you can.

CONTENTS

INTRODUCTION

Why do you want to learn assembly language? Most people do so out of a need to perform programming tasks that are not possible, or easy, with other languages. The popularity of the 8086/8088 family of microprocessors, exemplified by the sales figures of the IBM PC and others, makes it worthwhile to learn more about this particular micro. The microprocessor chip your computer uses will remain an abstraction unless you get down to the machine language level, but since no one programs in machine language, assembly language is the way to gain complete knowledge of the 8086/8088's capabilities.

Programming in assembly language allows you to control every aspect of the computer hardware. Many applications require capabilities that either are not possible or are inefficient with computer languages such as BASIC. You may be a professional computer-user who has a need for a laboratory control computer. Such real-time applications often require some assembly language programming. Whatever your reason for learning assembly language, the results are challenging and rewarding when your programs start to run. You will be in control.

This book is about programming the 8086/8088 microprocessor, not programming a specific computer using this chip. Some specifics about your computer and operating system will not be covered. Since you are probably experienced in using your computer for other applications, it would be a waste of time to attempt to cover all the small details. Instead, I will present the material in a general manner so it will be easy for you to dig up in your manuals the specifics for your particular machine.

Before we get started, let's review the steps required to write a program and run it. Assembly language, like high-level language programming, requires entering the *source code* into the computer. Unless all of your programming has been in BASIC, using the built-in editing features, you have probably used some form of text editor. It really doesn't matter which editor you use so long as you can create a source file for input to the assembler. An assembler is quite similar to a compiler in that it translates a source language into machine language.

The output from an assembler is called the *object code*. Normally this is machine language put into a special format that combines it with other object modules into an *executable image*. This file is essentially a picture of what goes into memory. When you finally run the program, this file is brought into memory and the microprocessor executes the instructions.

The operation of combining object modules is called *linking*. A special program called a linker performs this function. Figure 1 shows the steps used to produce an executable program. Details will differ from computer to computer. Your particular system may have a program similar to a linker that converts the output of your assembler into an executable form, but does not allow you to combine object modules. You should have no trouble learning the commands that perform these steps on your particular machine.

Step One. Text Editing

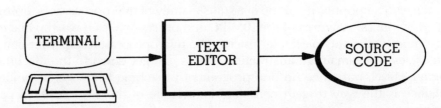

Step Two. Assembly

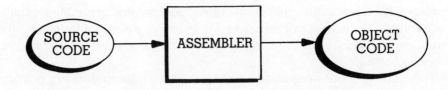

Step Three. Linking

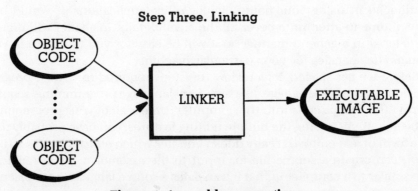

Figure 1. Assembler operation.

There are 8086/8088 assemblers available for a variety of computer systems, and it is not possible to present all their individual variations in this book. Intel Corporation, designer of the 8086/8088 microprocessor family, originated the assembly language. The assembler available from Intel, ASM86, is documented in Intel publication 121703-002, *ASM86 Language Reference Manual*. The most important task of the assembly language designer is to devise a set of symbolic names for each instruction the microprocessor can execute. These symbolic names are known as *mnemonics*. For example, an instruction to move data from one place to another has the mnemonic MOV.

Other popular assemblers are the ASM-86, available from Digital Research for its CP/M-86 operating system, and the assembler from Microsoft. The Microsoft assembler is used with MS-DOS and PC-DOS on the IBM PC. Both assemblers vary somewhat from the Intel assembler. The Microsoft is closer to the Intel version in functionality; however, the increased functionality is needed only for advanced programming, which is beyond the scope of this book.

In order to allow the greatest flexibility in the use of the assembler of your choice, this book will employ the standard Intel instruction mnemonics and will point out their differences from the Digital Research and Microsoft assemblers. Since most pieces of an assembly language program will be identical, regardless of the assembler used, you should not find it difficult to relate the material to your particular assembler.

CHAPTER 1

Number Systems

Throughout history mankind has used a variety of methods to represent numerical quantities. Early man used piles of stones, each stone representing one counted item. It soon became obvious that large numbers required a large number of stones. One solution to this problem was to use different sized stones. A single large stone could represent a pile of smaller stones. This system is similar to that used for denominations of paper currency. Such schemes work well for physical entities, like coins, paper currency, or stones; however, to represent quantities on paper, we would need to draw pictures of the piles of stones.

Decimal

Our decimal system is the end product of all these schemes. Rather than use different sized stones or piles of different numbers of stones, we use the Arabic numerals 0 to 9 and the relative position of these numerals to represent both the number of stones in a pile and the size of the stones. With the numerals, we can represent quantities from 0 to 9. By position we can represent any number of sizes. For example, the decimal number 23 can be thought of as representing 3 small stones and 2 larger stones. If each larger stone is equivalent to 10 small stones, the number is the equivalent of 23 small stones. This may seem obvious to most readers, but it is the basis of all the number systems we will study.

In the decimal number system, each digit's position represents a different power of 10. For example, the number 7458 is equivalent to:

$$7(10)^3+4(10)^2+5(10)^1+8(10)^0$$

The choice of 10 as the numerical base, or radix, as it is sometimes called, is arbitrary. We can create a number system using any base.

Binary

Virtually all computers use two as the base for numerical quantities. The choice of two as a base for computers is not arbitrary, however. Internally, the electrical elements, or gates, that collectively construct the computer are much easier to build if they are required to represent only two values or states. These are called *binary* state devices. Each element can represent only the values zero or one. Each one or zero is called a *bit*, or binary digit. In order to represent larger numbers, bit positions must be used. Binary numbers are based on powers of two rather than on powers of ten. For example, the binary number 1011 is equivalent to:

$$1(2)^3+0(2)^2+1(2)^1+1(2)^0$$

This value is equivalent to:

$$8+0+2+1 = 11$$

in decimal representation. You can easily determine that the positional values of the bits are:

$$(2)^0 = 1$$
$$(2)^1 = 2$$
$$(2)^2 = 4$$
$$(2)^3 = 8$$
$$(2)^4 = 16$$
.
.
.
$$(2)^{16} = 65,536$$
.
.
.
etc.

To convert a binary number to its decimal equivalent, we merely add up the appropriate powers of two. If the binary position contains a one, the decimal value of that bit position is added.

Conversions

Converting a decimal number to binary is not as simple as converting a binary number to decimal. One method is to work backwards. Look for the highest power of two that is not greater than the decimal number, place a one in the equivalent bit position, then subtract this value from the decimal number. Repeat this operation until the number is zero. Bit positions not used in this subtractive process are set at zero. For example, we can convert 57_{10} (57 in base 10) to binary by the following steps:

$$57 - 2^5 = 25$$
$$25 - 2^4 = 9$$
$$9 - 2^3 = 1$$
$$1 - 2^0 = 0 \text{ (finished)}$$

This gives us the binary number

$$1(2)^5+1(2)^4+1(2)^3+0(2)^2+0(2)^1+1(2)^0 = 111001_2$$

Another method can also be used. We can divide the original decimal number by two and check the remainder. If the remainder is one, a binary one is generated. We repeat this division by two until we obtain a zero. This method gives us the bits in reverse. In other words, we get 2^0 and then 2^1, etc. For example, use the same number as above:

```
57/2 = 28 R 1
28/2 = 14 R 0
14/2 = 7 R 0
7/2 = 3 R 1
3/2 = 1 R 1
1/2 = 0 R 1 (finished)
```

Reading the bits in reverse gives us 111001_2, the same answer we got before. The method you use is up to you.

SELF-CHECK
1) Binary numbers are based on powers of _____.
2) What is the decimal equivalent of the following binary numbers: 11100010, 111111, 10000000
3) Convert the following decimal numbers to binary: 126, 255, 100

1) Two.
2) 226, 63, 128
3) 1111110, 11111111, 1100100

These methods can be used to convert any number base to any other number base. However, unless converting from a decimal, we must do all the arithmetic in the number base of the number we are converting. This gets complicated. You are better off to convert the number to a decimal, then the decimal number to the new base. There are a few exceptions to this rule. One exception is when using the hexadecimal (hex) base and converting to or from binary. Since hex is used quite extensively with the 8086/8088 family, it is our next topic.

Hexadecimal

Hexadecimal, or base 16, uses positional values that are powers of 16. Each hex digit can take on 16 values. Since the decimal digits 0 through 9 will represent only 10 values, we need 6 additional symbols. The letters A through F are used to represent these additional values. Therefore, the hex digits are represented by 0, 1, 2, 3, 4, 5, 6, 7, 8, 9, A, B, C, D, E, and F. These correspond to the values from 0_{10} to 15_{10}. The positional values are:

```
(16)^0 = 1
(16)^1 = 16
(16)^2 = 256
(16)^3 = 4096
etc.
```

As you can see, these values increase rapidly. A hex number is usually larger than it looks. For example, $32BF_{16}$ is:

$$3(16)^3+2(16)^2+11(16)^1+15(16)^0$$
$$= 12,288+512+176+15 = 12,991_{10}$$

We can convert from decimal to hexadecimal by either method discussed above. For example, to convert 387_{10} to hex, we perform the following:

$$387/16 = 24 \text{ R } 3$$
$$24/16 = 1 \text{ R } 8$$
$$1/16 = 0 \text{ R } 1 \text{ (finished)}$$

Our result in hex is 183_{16}. Remember to list the hex digits in reverse order.

A nice property of hexadecimal numbers is that they can be converted to binary almost by inspection. Since $2^4=16$, there is a simple relationship present. Four binary digits grouped together can represent one hexadecimal digit. The binary values of 0000 through 1111 represent the hexadecimal digits 0 through F.

Hex	Binary	Hex	Binary
0	0000	8	1000
1	0001	9	1001
2	0010	A	1010
3	0011	B	1011
4	0100	C	1100
5	0101	D	1101
6	0110	E	1110
7	0111	F	1111

To convert from hex to binary, merely write the equivalent of each hex digit in binary. To convert $6E3C_{16}$ to binary, we would write:

```
  6    E    3    C
0110 1110 0011 1100
```

and our binary number is 110111000111100_2. We can go from binary to hex in the same manner. 111100001010_2 is $F0A_{16}$.

SELF-CHECK

1) Convert the following binary numbers to hexadecimal: 11111111, 10000, 11000101
2) Convert the following hexadecimal numbers to binary: 55, AB, EE
3) What is the decimal equivalent of the following hexadecimal numbers: FF, 55, DE

1) FF, 10, C5
2) 01010101, 10101011, 11101110
3) 255, 85, 222

Arithmetic in Binary and Hexadecimal

We can perform the normal arithmetic operations of addition, subtraction, multiplication, and division in any number base. Addition and subtraction are simple if we remember that a carry or borrow may be required. If the sum of two digits equals or exceeds the number base, a carry is generated. The value used as the carry or borrow is equal to the number base. For example, if we add two binary numbers together, we generate a carry if the sum of any two bits and a possible carry is equal to or greater than two. Adding 1100101_2 to 0111101_2 gives us:

```
  1100101
+ 0111101
 10100010
```

Let's try adding $72A8_{16}$ to $1F08_{16}$.

```
  72A8
+ 1F08
  91B0
```

Subtraction is only slightly more difficult. If the individual digits cannot be subtracted from one another, we need to borrow from the next higher digit position. In other words, if the minuend (top digit) is less than the subtrahend (bottom digit), we need a borrow. In binary we always borrow a value of two. This borrow is added to the minuend, then the subtraction is performed on the two digits. To adjust for the borrow, just as for a carry, we must add one to the subtrahend in the next higher digit position. For example, in binary

```
  1111        1001
- 0110      - 0110
  1001        0011
```

or hexadecimal

```
  55F2
- 4A63
  0B8F
```

Hand calculations involving multiplication or division are rarely performed by programmers. However, conventional hand methods can be used. The basic principles used for addition and subtraction are applied. Although I will not cover multiplication or division, readers can try some examples and verify their results by converting to decimal, then repeating the multiplication or division in the decimal number base.

SELF-CHECK

1) Perform the following binary additions:

   a)   110000
      + 001111

   b)   01111
      + 11100

2) Perform the following hexadecimal additions:

   a)   FFAA
      + A100

   b)   0123
      + A5EE

3) Perform the following binary subtractions:

   a)   11111
      − 00101

   b)   11001
      − 10000

4) Perform the following hexadecimal subtractions:

   a)   FFFF
      − AAAA

   b)   12AA
      − 02AB

1) a) 111111
   b) 101011
2) a) 1A0AA
   b) A711
3) a) 11010
   b) 01001
4) a) 55555
   b) 0FFF

Bits, Bytes, Words, and Double Words

In our discussion of numbers we have not indicated how large our numbers can be. If you write a very large number on paper, the size of the number is limited only by the size of the paper. This is not the case with computers. The internal representations of numbers are restricted to certain sizes. Since binary is normally used as the internal representation of numbers on computers, the maximum size of a binary number is determined by the number of binary digits, or bits, of the number.

Many computers are organized around groups of eight bits. A group of eight bits is called a *byte*. The size of memory on many computers is measured in bytes. We might say a computer has 64 thousand bytes of memory. This is equivalent to 512 thousand bits. Modern computers often have memory sizes in the millions of bytes. A megabyte (MB) is equal to a million bytes. A single byte is normally used to represent a single character of textual information. If we have a 2MB memory, we can store 2 million characters of information. If we assume approximately 60 characters per line of printed material and 50 lines per page, this is equivalent to over 650 pages.

Bytes can be grouped together. For most computers, including the 8086/8088 family, two bytes grouped together form a *word*. A word is therefore equal to 16 bits or to 4 hexadecimal digits. We can also have double words, or 32 bits, and even quadwords. We will deal primarily with bytes and words with assembly language programming.

Two's Complement

So far in our discussion of number representations, we have dealt only with positive numbers. A method for representing negative numbers in the computer must be introduced. You have already learned that numbers are represented internally by binary digits. If we are to use the conventional minus sign (−) to indicate a negative number, we must devise a way of including this minus sign with the number itself. But how does a minus sign translate into binary? Since numbers are either positive or negative, we can use a single binary digit. A negative number can be indicated by using an extra bit, rather than a minus sign. This may not work as well on paper, but it is essential for a computer's internal representations.

Numeric quantities are normally restricted to fixed sizes. They can be a single byte, a word, or some multiple number of words or bytes. It is not practical to append an extra "sign" bit to a fixed unit of storage, such as a byte. Normally the central processing unit (CPU) is restricted to manipulating integral numbers of bytes. This extra bit would force the use of an extra complete byte. The solution is to sacrifice one of our bits for use as the sign bit. The size of the largest number we can represent is reduced, but we can now represent the same number of positive as of negative numbers.

By convention, if a number is negative, include a sign bit equal to one. The sign bit is normally the leftmost, or high-order, bit of the number. The simplest technique would be to indicate the magnitude of the number in the remaining bits, then set the sign bit to either 1 or 0 to indicate a negative or positive number. This representation, called *sign magnitude,* has been used on older computers. It has a number of disadvantages, the most prominent being the fact that for a programmer both a positive and negative zero exist. Both 10000000_2 and 00000000_2 are zero values for a single byte number. Suffice it to say that a better method is needed.

Virtually all modern computers, including microprocessors, use a representation called *two's complement*. The sign bit is still used to indicate whether a number is positive or negative, but the remaining bits do not directly indicate the magnitude of the number if it is a negative number. To represent a negative number in two's complement, we first form the one's complement of the number in its binary form. The one's complement is merely the number with all the one bits converted to zeros, and all the zero bits converted to ones. The one's complement of 01100011_2 is 10011100_2. So far this is quite simple. We are almost finished. To get the two's complement, we add one to the one's complement. We perform this addition just as in the previous examples. To complete the conversion of our example, we get:

$$
\begin{array}{r}
10011100 \\
+\ 00000001 \\
\hline
10011101
\end{array}
$$

Let's convert 89_{10} to -89_{10} using two's complement. First we must convert 89_{10} to binary: $89_{10} = 01011001_2$. Now form the one's complement, 10100110_2. Finally, to get the two's complement, we add one. Our result is $-89_{10} = 10100111_2$.

The nice property of two's complement numbers is that we can add them together without concern for the sign. We do not have to perform any conversion. As a simple example, we should be able to add 89_{10} and -89_{10} and obtain a zero result.

$$
\begin{array}{ll}
\ \ 01011001 & 89_{10} \\
+\ 10100111 & -89_{10} \\
\hline
\ \ 00000000 & 0_{10}
\end{array}
$$

We ignore any carry that is out of the sign bit position.

To subtract two numbers in two's complement, we merely negate the subtrahend and then add. This operation is performed whether the subtrahend is positive or negative.

SELF-CHECK

1) How many bits are there in a byte?
2) How many bytes are contained in an 8086/8088 word?
3) The 8086/8088 uses what method to represent negative numbers?
4) Which bit is the sign bit?
5) If a number is negative, what is the binary value of the sign bit?
6) Convert the binary number 00111101 to an equivalent negative number.
7) What is the decimal equivalent of 11110000 in signed binary?
8) What is the equivalent of −100 decimal in a signed hexadecimal byte?

1) 8
2) 2
3) Two's complement.
4) The high order bit.
5) One.
6) 11000011
7) −16
8) 9C

ASCII Character Codes

In order to represent character information in the computer's memory, we must find a way to convert the character set to numeric values. Over the years a number of different coding schemes have been used. Currently almost all computers (IBM mainframes, etc.) use EBCDIC (Extended Binary-Coded Decimal Interchange Code) or ASCII (American Standard Code for Information Interchange). Since ASCII is used by virtually all microcomputers on the market today, we will confine our discussion to ASCII. The 8086/8088 really doesn't care what code is used to represent characters. Rather, the terminal devices (at the hardware level) and the software used with the terminal require compatibility. If you type a key on your terminal, the terminal generates the numeric value corresponding to the character. If the software you are running expects the ASCII code for this character, your terminal must be set up for ASCII.

Appendix A lists the ASCII character codes. Since we would like upper- and lower-case alphabetic characters, the digits 0 through 9, and the common punctuation marks, we need a minimum of 75 to 100 different numeric values. A single byte is adequate to represent the integers 0 through 255, which is sufficient for 256 different characters. The ASCII code uses only the values 0 through 127, corresponding to 7 of the 8 bits in a byte.

The integers 0_{10} through 31_{10} are reserved for special nonprinting codes. These include the carriage controls such as CR (carriage return), LF (line feed), and HT (horizontal tab). There are other *control character codes* that are of general interest but that are not necessarily available on all terminals. For example, a BEL (bell) might sound a beep on your terminal, or a VT (vertical tab) might be implemented. Other codes less than 32_{10} are used for a variety of purposes, including the protocols for data communications.

One special character should be mentioned. The DEL (delete) code, 127_{10}, sometimes called a rubout, is most commonly used by software to indicate the deletion of the last character typed. Some software uses the BS (back-space) character to perform this same operation. You should note that these are really two different character codes, 8_{10} vs. 127_{10}, and the interpretation as to what, if anything, these characters do is up to the software.

Some computers and terminals have incorporated additional characters as an extension to the standard ASCII character set. By allowing codes above

127_{10}, an additional 128_{10} characters can be specified. These might be a foreign language or special graphics used by certain terminals. The IBM PC makes extensive use of such an extended character set. You should be aware that these special character sets are not part of the ASCII standard. When you use these codes, your programs will not necessarily be useful on *all* computers, even those that use the 8086/8088 microprocessor.

SELF-TEST

1) What number bases are convenient to use when programming the 8086/8088? *Binary out Hex*
2) Hexadecimal numbers use what number base? *16*
3) What number base is used internally by the 8086/8088? *2*
4) Convert the following decimal numbers to binary and hexadecimal:
   a) 200   *100 RD   50 RO   25 RO   12 R1   6 R0   3 R0   1 R1   0 R1   1100 1000*
   b) 5
   c) 65000
5) Convert the following unsigned binary numbers to decimal:
   a) 11010101   *128 + 64 + 16 + 4 + 1 = 213*
   b) 00001110   *8 + 4 + 2 = 14*
   c) 11100000110   *128 + 64 + 32 + 4 + 2 = 230*
6) Convert the following unsigned hexadecimal numbers to decimal:
   a) ABCD
   b) 123
   c) FF
7) Convert the following hexadecimal numbers to binary:
   a) FEAA   *1111 1110 1010 1010*
   b) 123A   *0001 0010 0011 1010*
   c) 0100   *0000 0001 0000 0000*
8) Convert the following binary numbers to hexadecimal:
   a) 1100110001   *331*
   b) 00010000   *10*
   c) 11110111   *F7*
9) Perform the following signed binary additions:
   a) 11111000 + 00111111
   b) 00010001 + 01000000
   c) 11111100 + 00000011
10) Perform the following signed binary subtractions:
    a) 11100000 − 00000001
    b) 00111000 − 11111111
    c) 10101010 − 00010101
11) What is the range of the ASCII codes that are printable?
12) Does the 8086/8088 interpret the ASCII character codes?

---

1) Decimal, binary, and hexadecimal.
2) 16

3) Binary.

4) a) 11001000_2 $C8_{16}$

   b) 101_2 5_{16}

   c) 111110111101000_2 $FDE8_{16}$

5) a) 213

   b) 14

   c) 1798

6) a) 43981

   b) 288

   c) 255

7) a) 1111111010101010

   b) 1001000111010

   c) 100000000

8) a) 331

   b) 10

   c) F7

9) a) 100110111

   b) 01010001

   c) 11111111

10) a) 11011111

    b) 00111001

    c) 10010101

11) 33_{10} through 126_{10}, assuming that space 32_{10} does not print.

12) No. Input and output devices and software interpret the ASCII codes.

CHAPTER 2

Microcomputer Architecture

Before we begin to discuss assembly language, we should take time to explore the world of the microcomputer. Just what is a microcomputer? As the name implies, it is a small computer. This should not mislead you into thinking that a microcomputer cannot be a powerful computing tool. In fact, the microcomputers of today are as powerful as the minicomputers and mainframe computers of a few years ago. The reduction in size has been a direct consequence of the development of integrated circuits (chips) that contain the functional equivalent of many thousands of transistors.

A microprocessor is an integrated circuit that is the basic functional building block of the microcomputer. Figure 2 shows the organization of a basic microcomputer system. The CPU is the microprocessor chip itself. Electrically connected to the CPU chip is memory. Memory can be of various sizes, for example, a maximum of one million bytes for the 8086/8088 microprocessor. Also connected to the CPU are input and output (I/O) devices that allow the CPU to communicate with the outside world through a terminal as well as through other information storage devices, such as floppy disks and magnetic tapes.

The Intel Family

In this book you will be learning assembly language programming for the Intel iAPX 86,88/186,188 family of microprocessors, which includes the 8086/8088 and the newer 80186/80188 microprocessors. The difference between the 8086 and the 8088 microprocessors is in how many bytes are transferred to or from memory at one time. The 8086 transfers two bytes; the 8088 transfers only one byte. This difference affects the performance of the microprocessors. The 8086 performs somewhat faster than the 8088. There is no difference so far as the programmer is concerned. Since the instructions on both microprocessors are identical, it makes no difference which chip your computer is using.

The 80186 and 80188 are improved versions of the 8086 and 8088. They contain certain additional hardware features, such as programmable timers

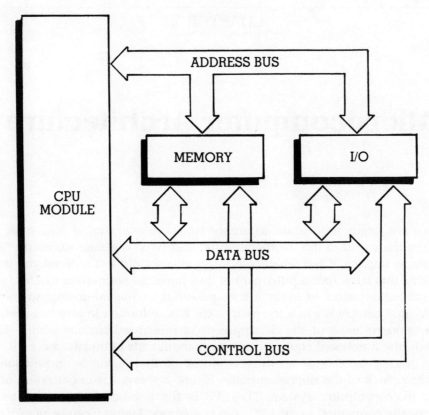

Figure 2. Organization of a simple microcomputer system.
(Courtesy of Intel)

and ten new instructions. These additional instructions will be covered in Chapter 14. When I speak of the 8086/8088, I will generally mean the entire family of microprocessors, including the 80186 and 80188.

Intel has recently introduced a new microprocessor, the iAPX 286 or 80286, a very advanced CPU, with capabilities that set it apart from the other chips in the iAPX 86 family. These capabilities are mainly in the area of memory management. They make it possible for the 80286 to be used for the design of microcomputers that allow multiple simultaneous users. A special chapter will be devoted to introducing these new features.

Before we get started on assembly language programming, it is essential to look at the 8086/8088 microprocessor architecture. We will not discuss every detail of the actual machine language used by the CPU, but we must know enough about the structure of memory and the internal CPU registers to use assembly language.

As you are probably aware from your experience with a high-level programming language, such as BASIC or PASCAL, all information in the computer's memory and all information acted on by the CPU must be represented as numbers. This includes textual information, which is represented by numeric equivalents for each character as governed by an appropriate character set. You will learn more about character manipulation in future chapters.

The instructions of the 8086/8088 microprocessor are designed to manipulate numeric information in a variety of ways. Data can be moved from one place to another in the computer's memory, or data can be moved from memory to registers contained in the microprocessor chip. Registers are special places to store and manipulate data. They are like memory locations, except that they operate at much higher speeds and serve special purposes for the CPU. The most important use of the registers is in performing arithmetic operations. The 8086/8088 is capable of performing the normal arithmetic operations on integer numbers, such as addition, subtraction, multiplication, and division, as well as logical operations. Logical operations allow manipulation of individual bits of the data. You will soon see how logical operations can be very useful.

Some instructions do not manipulate data but are used to control the flow of your program. Often you will want to repeat an operation many times. Rather than repeat the instructions over and over when you write your program, you can use the control instructions so that the microprocessor will automatically repeat a group of instructions that you have written only once.

Since a computer program would be useless without a way to get information into and out of the computer, the 8086/8088 microprocessor includes instructions for inputting and outputting data to external devices, such as a video terminal or printer. Even though your computer may include a built-in terminal (screen and keyboard), it is really an I/O device as far as the CPU is concerned.

SELF-CHECK
1) What are the three main parts of a microcomputer?
2) What is the difference between the 8086 and the 8088?
3) Are registers faster or slower than memory?

---

1) CPU, Memory, and I/O.
2) The 8086 transfers two bytes of data to and from memory, while the 8088 only transfers one byte.
3) Much faster.

Memory

The memory used with the 8086/8088 consists of a number of cells. Each cell, or location, will hold one 8-bit number or byte. Memory cells are numbered starting at zero, up to the maximum allowable amount of memory. The 8086/8088 allows a maximum of one megabyte of memory. This is actually $1,048,576_{10}$ locations or addresses. Figure 3 shows the concept of memory cells and their corresponding addresses.

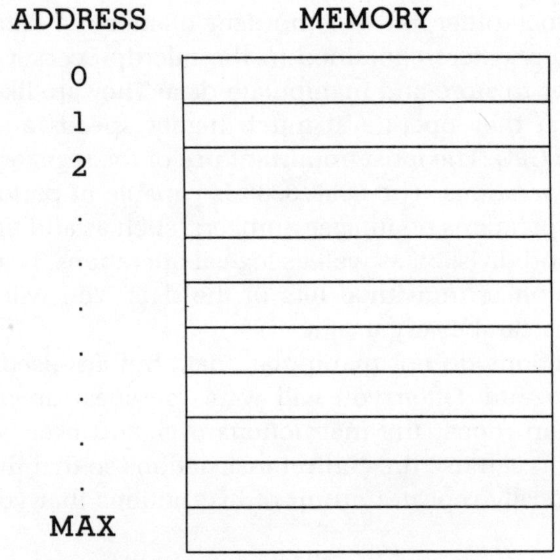

ADDRESS   MEMORY

0

1

2

.

.

.

.

.

MAX

Figure 3. Memory organization.

A program consists of instructions and data. Since everything in memory is a number, careful organization is required to prevent the computer from interpreting instructions as data or data as instructions. This is normally the responsibility of the programmer. However, the 8086/8088, unlike many microprocessors, provides help in organizing the instructions and data of your program in memory by using what is known as a segmented memory organization. In addition to allowing the separation of your instructions and data, this segmentation also allows a full one megabyte of memory to be referenced. Normally only $65,536_{10}$ locations can be referenced with microprocessors such as the Intel 8080 or the Motorola 6800. This amount of memory is also referred to as 64K, where K indicates $1,024_{10}$.

Memory in the 8086/8088 can be segmented into four regions, each region corresponding to a different segment. The instructions of your program reside in the CODE segment. Your data would normally be in the DATA segment. Two additional segments are provided, a STACK segment and an EXTRA segment. The use of these two additional segments will be explained shortly. Figure 4 shows a possible division of your memory into these four segments. Each of the four segments can be of any length up to 64K bytes. In fact, they can overlap each other, which, under certain circumstances, is desirable.

MEMORY

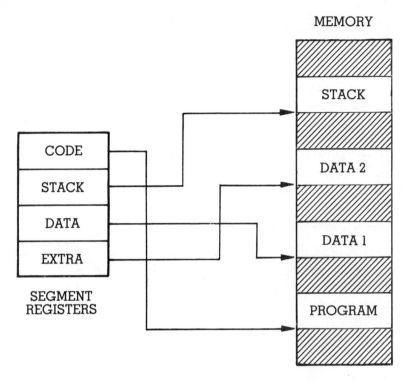

Figure 4. Memory segments. (Courtesy of Intel)

To reference one megabyte of memory requires an address that can be up to 20 bits in length. Addresses used by the 8086/8088 instructions are only 16 bits in length; $2^{16} = 65,536$ while $2^{20} = 1,048,576$. In order to make up the difference, memory is divided into 16-byte chunks. These chunks are known as *paragraphs*. The starting address of a paragraph is always a multiple of 16. The first 5 paragraph addresses in hexadecimal and decimal are:

Hex	Dec
00000	0
00010	16
00020	32
00030	48
00040	64

As you can see, the low-order or rightmost four bits of the paragraph addresses are always zero. Remember from Chapter 1 that each hexadecimal digit corresponds to four binary digits. Therefore, a paragraph address can actually be represented as a 16-bit number with four low-order binary zeros added at the right. The 8086/8088 utilizes this fact and provides four 16-bit registers to hold the starting paragraph number for each of the four segments. These are known as *segment base registers* and are designated CS, DS, SS, and ES. They correspond to the CODE, DATA, STACK, and EXTRA segments. When an instruction references memory, the paragraph address of the proper segment is added to the 16-bit address provided by the instruction. The 16-bit address provided by the instruction is actually an *offset* into the segment. The result is a 20-bit address in the actual physical memory.

As an example, suppose an instruction is referencing location 1234H (1234_{16}) in the DATA segment. Further, let us suppose that the register holding the paragraph number of the DATA segment currently contains 2000H. The actual physical memory location referenced would then be 21234H. This is computed as follows:

Paragraph address of DATA segment	20000
Offset in DATA segment	+ 1234
	21234

Notice that a hexadecimal zero has been implicitly appended to the paragraph number, 2000H. The actual location of this paragraph in physical memory is 20000H.

CPU Registers

The 8086/8088 and 80186/80188 contain a total of fourteen registers that the programmer is able to access. Figure 5 shows the entire set of registers for the 8086/8088. We have already discussed the four segment registers, CS, DS, SS, and ES. Of the ten remaining registers, eight are known as general purpose registers, and the two remaining are status and control registers.

Each of the eight general purpose registers is 16 bits long. They actually fall into two groups of four registers: the data registers and the pointer/index registers. Let's discuss the four data registers first. They are the AX, BX, CX, and DX registers. Each one will hold a 16-bit number. We normally use the data registers to perform arithmetic. They are all essentially equal when used with most instructions; however, implicit use is made of specific registers for certain instructions. This will be clear when we cover the instructions of the 8086/8088 in detail.

You will probably notice that the AX, BX, CX, and DX registers are broken into two halves, with each half a single byte. We don't really have two new registers, only a division of the four 16-bit registers into separate pieces. The nice feature is that we can use either half independently. As you can see, the AX register is broken down into the AH and AL halves (the H and L refer to the high- and low-order bytes). Similarly BX, CX, and DX have a BH, BL, CH, CL, DH, and DL. Each of these registers will hold an 8-bit number. Except under special circumstances, if we use one of these 8-bit registers, we can't use its 16-bit parent at the same time. This is because the eight bits are in common and can't hold two different values.

DATA REGISTERS

	7	07	0
AX	AH	AL	
BX	BH	BL	
CX	CH	CL	
DX	DH	DL	

POINTER AND INDEX REGISTERS

	15	0	
SP			STACK POINTER
BP			BASE POINTER
SI			SOURCE INDEX
DI			DESTINATION INDEX

SEGMENT REGISTERS

	15	0	
CS			CODE
DS			DATA
SS			STACK
ES			EXTRA

Figure 5. CPU registers. (Courtesy of Intel)

The pointer and index registers consist of the Stack Pointer (SP), the Base Pointer (BP), and the Source and Destination Index registers (SI and DI). These are 16-bit-only registers. They can be used for arithmetic operations, but their real power is related to their use with the powerful addressing modes of the 8086/8088. The addressing mode refers to the particular method used to calculate the memory locations or addresses that your program references. We will cover addressing modes in detail in Chapter 9.

The remaining two registers are the Instruction Pointer (IP) and the Status Word, or Flags, register. Neither of these registers is referenced directly by your program. The Instruction Pointer, or program counter as it is sometimes called, is used to contain the memory location of the next instruction to be executed. This is actually the offset within the code segment, as determined by the contents of the CS segment register. In other words, the 20-bit number formed by the contents of the IP and CS registers actually specifies the physical memory address of the next instruction to be executed.

The Status Word, or Flags, register consists of three control flags and six status flags. The status flags are used to record specific characteristics of arithmetic and of logical instructions. For example, the zero flag is set if the result of a calculation is zero. The control flags are used to control certain modes of the CPU, such as whether hardware interrupts are allowed. We will discuss the status flags in detail in Chapter 5.

SELF-CHECK

1) How much memory is allowed with the 8086/8088?   *1.0 m*
2) What are the four memory segments?   *Code Data Stack Extra*
3) What is the maximum size of a segment?   *64K*
4) What are the 16-bit general purpose registers?   *AX, BX, CX, DX*

1) One megabyte.
2) CODE, DATA, STACK, and EXTRA.
3) 64K
4) AX, BX, CX, DX, SP, BP, SI, and DI.

Representation of Instructions and Data in Memory

One of the reasons for using assembly language is to free the programmer from worry about the exact representation of instructions and data in memory. However, a programmer usually finds an occasion when such knowledge is useful.

Remember that memory consists of an array of individually addressable bytes. If the data we wish to store in memory consists of only a single byte, there is no question as to how it is represented, only where. If, however, the data consists of a word or instruction containing more than one byte, it is not clear how this information is stored. Word data (16 bits) is always stored with the high-order byte in the higher memory address. This means that if we were reading a dump of memory, word data would appear *byte flipped*. In other words, the number 1234H would appear in memory as 3412H. If you are careful, this normally doesn't cause a problem. It gives the computer no trouble at all.

Instructions consist of one or more bytes. The first byte is always the operation code, or *opcode*. This specifies what the particular instruction is. For example, a divide instruction is either an $F6_{16}$ or an $F7_{16}$, depending on whether we are dividing by a byte or a word. Many instructions are actually represented by several different opcodes, each specifying a version of the instruction.

A second byte is needed with some instructions to further specify the instruction's action. With a few exceptions, this second byte is used to indicate the operand types used by the instruction. Operands may be registers, immediate data, or variables located in memory. If immediate data or a memory location requires specification, one or more additional bytes are needed. Immediate data is data that is part of the instruction bytes themselves. This will become clearer as we get into actual programs in Chapter 4.

SELF-TEST

1) How many bytes does a paragraph contain? *16*
2) What is the maximum number of paragraphs that 8086/8088 memory can contain? *64K*
3) What four 16-bit registers are actually register pairs, and what are the 8-bit registers? *AX, BX, CX, DX, AH, AL, BH, BL, CH, CL*
4) What two registers are used to form the 20-bit address of the next instruction? *CS IP*
5) Is 16-bit data stored with the high-order byte first? *No*
6) Are all instructions the same number of bytes? *No*

---

1) 16
2) 1 megabyte of memory is allowed with the 8086/8088. Since a paragraph is 16 bytes, 65,536 paragraphs constitute this 1 megabyte.
3) AX, BX, CX, and DX consist of the pairs AH, AL, BH, BL, CH, CL, DH, and DL.
4) IP and CS.
5) No, the high-order byte is the higher address and is therefore stored second.
6) No, an instruction can be one or more bytes. The first byte is the opcode byte.

Low

↓

High

CHAPTER 3

Assembler Source Format

The assembler processes the source program line by line. A line of the source program can represent several things. It can be translated into a machine instruction, can generate an element or elements of data to be placed in memory, or the line may provide information only to the assembler itself. The lines of the source program are sometimes referred to as source statements.

Regardless of the use of a particular line of the source program, the format of each line is relatively standard. The general format of a source line is divided into four fields as follows:

[label] operation [operand] [;comment]

Not all four fields must appear on all lines. Brackets, [], have been used to indicate fields that are optional. The comment field is always optional, but the label and/or operand fields may be required, depending on the contents of the operation field. Unless a source line consists solely of a comment field, the operation field is required.

A field consists of one or more tokens. A *token* is the smallest meaningful unit of information that the assembler uses. Tokens are identifiers or numeric constants. The symbolic names of the machine instructions are an example of identifiers. Separators are sometimes needed to mark the end of a token. All 8086/8088 assemblers recognize the space character as a separator. Most assemblers also recognize the tab character as a separator and treat it as a space. Separators are used, too, to mark the end of one source line field and the beginning of the next. While a space or tab is not always needed, its use adds to the readability of the program. Generally, where one space or tab is allowed, you may use more than one. One or more spaces or tabs are used to separate the fields of the source statement.

Delimiters are special characters that can serve to mark the end of a token, but they also have a special meaning. Punctuation characters, such as commas, periods, colons, etc., are examples of delimiters. In most cases a separator can be used with a delimiter to enhance readability.

Figure 6 is an excerpt from a sample program that we will use to discuss further the format of assembler source lines. As you can see, the program

```
;THIS PROGRAM INPUTS TEN INTEGERS AND THEN
;PRINTS THE LARGEST
;
COUNT    EQU    10               ;INTEGERS TO COMPARE
;
         MOV    CX,COUNT    ;INITIALIZE LOOP
         MOV    BIGONE,0    ;SET LARGEST TO ZERO
NEXT:    CALL   INDEC       ;INPUT A NUMBER
         CMP    AX,BIGONE   ;COMPARE WITH CURRENT
         JLE    L           ; < OR =
         MOV    BIGONE,AX   ; >, WE HAVE NEW ONE
L:       LOOP   NEXT        ;LOOP FOR NEXT NUMBER
         MOV    AX,BIGONE   ;SET UP FOR OUTPUT
         CALL   OUTDEC      ;OUTPUT THE LARGEST NUMBER
         HLT                ;ALL DONE HERE
         . . .
         . . .
INDEC:   . . .              ;INPUT PROCEDURE
         . . .
OUTDEC:  . . .              ;OUTPUT PROCEDURE
         . . .
         . . .
BIGONE   DW     0           ;CURRENT LARGEST
         . . .
         . . .
```

Figure 6. Sample Program.

consists mainly of character sequences that look like English words separated by punctuation. These character sequences are known as *identifiers.* The rules for creating identifiers vary slightly, but the following rules work with almost all assemblers:

1. The first character must be alphabetic (A . . . Z, a . . . z).
2. Any additional characters may be either alphabetic or one of the digits (0 . . . 9).
3. Only the first 31 characters are significant; the rest are ignored.

SELF-CHECK

1) Does every line of the source program have to represent a machine instruction? *No*
2) Is a comment required on every source line? *No*
3) What is the smallest unit of information that the assembler uses? *Token*
4) What characters can be used to separate the fields of the source statement? *space, tab, period, comma, etc*
5) Which of the following are legal identifiers: FOO, 5ORANGES, F1040, FULL(BYTE

1) No. Source line may be used to create data items or to provide information for the assembler.
2) No. Comments are always optional, but it is a good idea to provide as many comments as possible.
3) A token. Tokens are identifiers or numbers.
4) Spaces or tabs.
5) FOO is legal; 5ORANGES is not legal since it starts with a digit; F1040 is legal; FULL(BYTE is not legal since the (is not a legal character in an identifier.

The Label Field

The label field always contains a symbol formed with the standard rules for identifiers. If a label is present, it is used to associate the symbol with a value. This value may represent a variable's location in memory, a constant, or the location of the instruction in the operation field.

Variables represent data stored at particular locations in memory. Associated with each variable are three attributes:

1. The segment containing the variable.
2. The offset within the segment where the variable is located.
3. The type of variable.

The variable type tells how many bytes are needed to store the data.

A symbol in the label field can be made to represent a numeric constant. Anywhere this symbol appears in your program, it is interpreted as if you had written the constant itself. For example, you could define the symbol MAX to represent the constant 1000.

A symbol in the label field can also be used to specify the memory location of an instruction. This is a *true label*. Although the first field is called the label field, only the symbols present in the label field of a source line that translates into a machine instruction are the true labels of an 8086/8088 assembly language program. These symbols must be delimited with a semicolon.

The Operation Field

The operation field contains either a machine instruction or an assembler directive. Each machine instruction has a special symbol, or *mnemonic*, associated with it. If a particular machine instruction is desired, the proper mnemonic must be placed in the operation field. Assembler directives have symbolic names that are different from the machine instructions. The assembler is thus able to differentiate between a machine instruction and a directive.

If a machine instruction is placed in the operation field, the assembler will generate the appropriate bytes to be placed in memory, corresponding to the translation of the source statement. Assembler directives may or may not generate bytes to be stored in memory. Some directives merely control the format of the assembly listing, or provide information about the segments that are to be used. Directives are also used to define symbols. We will discuss assembler directives in Chapter 6.

The Operand Field

Many machine instructions, as well as assembler directives, require one or more operands. The operand field is used to provide these. Individual operands can consist of constants, variables, or special symbols. Expressions made up of constants, variables, and special symbols are also permitted. The rules for making up expressions vary slightly from assembler to assembler. Standard arithmetic expressions, such as

COUNT+5

are allowed by all assemblers.

If more than one operand is required with an instruction or assembler directive, the operands are separated by a comma. This comma is a delimiter, and you do not need a space before or after its use. For example,

ADD   NUMBER1,NUMBER2

results in two variables, NUMBER1 and NUMBER2, being added together, with the result placed in the variable NUMBER1.

The 8086/8088 microprocessor uses a variety of addressing modes. In order to specify the particular addressing mode desired, the operands are combined with special delimiters. For example,

MOV   AX, [BX]

indicates the register indirect mode of addressing used with the BX register. The left and right square brackets are the special delimiters used to indicate this type of addressing. You will learn more about the 8086/8088 addressing modes in Chapter 9.

The Comment Field

The comment field is used to provide information for the programmer and for others who may examine the program. Assembly language is not self-documenting. Often, even the programmer, if away from it for some time, may have difficulty in remembering exactly how the program works. Comments are best used to provide a running description of the program's operation. Comments help those who may have to maintain the program in the future and they can also be used to provide information on using a particular program.

A comment can be used on every line of the program. A semicolon must precede the comment. When the assembler scans the semicolon, it ignores the remainder of the line. Comments are not interpreted or used in any way by the assembler. A comment may be the only thing on a source line. Although most assemblers allow comment lines to start in any column, it is general practice to start the comment line with the semicolon in column one. See the comments in Figure 6.

SELF-CHECK

1) What are the three attributes of a variable?
2) What two things can the operation field contain?
3) What special character starts a comment?
4) What special character is used to separate multiple operands in the operand field?

====

1) Segment, offset, and type.
2) A machine instruction or an assembler directive.
3) A semicolon.
4) A comma.

Choosing Symbols

When you need to select a new symbol for use as a constant, variable, or label for an instruction, you are free to create arbitrary symbols if you adhere to the rules for creating an identifier. However, some assemblers do not allow you to create symbols that are the same as the instruction mnemonics or assembler directives. These reserved symbols are known as the keywords of the assembler. Even though it may be clear when a symbol is used as an instruction rather than as a variable, some assemblers are not that smart. Even if your assembler can make this distinction, it is a good practice to avoid using keywords. Consult your assembler manual. You can usually find a table of all the keywords that the assembler recognizes.

It is good programming practice to choose symbols that have a meaning related to their use in the program. For example, if you use a variable to keep track of a count, why not name it COUNT? Short symbols like I, J, or N can be used, but they don't tell us much. Labels for instructions can indicate the function of a particular portion of the program. The label READDATA clearly indicates the reading of some data. The label L23 does not convey any meaning. Although many assemblers allow extremely long identifiers, keeping them to eight characters or less is standard practice. Most programmers line up the source line fields on tab stops set at every eight columns. Long identifiers make lining up the fields difficult unless a lot of extra space is used to accommodate the largest symbols.

Constants

A *constant* is a value that does not change during program assembly or execution. Two types of constants can be used: integers and character strings.

Integer constants are numeric quantities that can be represented by 16 bits or less. You will remember from Chapter 1 that numbers can be represented in various number bases. If a constant is specified without indicating this base or radix, it is assumed to be in the decimal number base. To indicate that a constant is written in a number base other than 10, we can terminate the number with a radix indicator. The radix indicators we can use are:

Indicator	Base
B	2
O	8
Q	8
D	10
H	16

A binary constant would naturally consist of only 1s and 0s, followed by an upper- or lowercase B. If we try to write a binary constant with other than 1s and 0s, we produce an error. A problem exists with hexadecimal constants that does not exist with the other number bases. If the first hex digit is a letter (A–F), it is not possible to tell whether we mean a numeric constant or a symbol. For example, AH could be either the number A_{16} or the identifier AH. If we want to write hexadecimal constants that begin with A to H, we add an extra 0 digit at the beginning of the number. We would then write 0AH if we meant the hexadecimal constant. The following are all valid constants:

```
1234            1234₁₀
1234H           1234₁₆
1100111001B     110011100₁₂
0FFFFH          FFFF₁₆
377Q            377₈
```

Character string constants are ASCII character strings delimited by apostrophes. A character string constant must appear entirely on one line. Any valid "printing" characters from the ASCII character set are allowed. For example:

'Hello there.'

is a character string of length 12. The two apostrophes are not included in the string. What do we do if we want an apostrophe? We can't just place one in the middle of the string. That would terminate the string. If we want a single apostrophe, we write two apostrophes. For example:

'Don''t give up the ship.'

is actually the string, "Don't give up the ship.".

If a string is one or two characters long, it has either an 8-bit or a 16-bit numeric value. If it is longer than two characters, it is merely the string of bytes with the appropriate ASCII values. Both upper- and lower-case characters can be used in character strings.

SELF-TEST

1) When is it legal to leave out the operation field of a source statement?
2) What are the four fields of a source statement?
3) What is a mnemonic?
4) Can a comment precede an instruction on a source line?
5) Tab stops are normally set up for how many columns?
6) Which of the following are legal constants: 12345, ABCDH, 0F00H, 345B, 777Q ?
7) What is the character string constant for "Let's quote ' ' '"?

1) When the source line consists solely of a comment.
2) Label, operation, operand, and comment.
3) The symbolic representation of a machine instruction.
4) No, the remainder of the line is ignored following the semicolon.
5) 8
6) 12345 is a legal decimal constant; ABCDH is not legal because it cannot be differentiated from an identifier; 0F00H is a legal hex constant; 345B is not a legal binary constant because only the digits 0 and 1 can be used with binary constants; 777Q is a legal octal constant.
7) 'Let''s quote """"'

CHAPTER 4

Getting Started

In order to write a program in assembly language, you must develop a familiarity with the machine instructions of the 8086/8088. These instructions can be grouped together according to function. For example, there are instructions that are used to move data between memory and the registers; another group of instructions performs the standard arithmetic operations, like addition, subtraction, multiplication, and division. Still other groups perform only control functions, such as looping. Rather than present all the instructions from each group in order, I will offer some key instructions from each group so that you can start to understand complete programs without being overwhelmed.

After you have completed this chapter, you will know enough to write and execute simple 8086/8088 assembly language programs. It is important that you take the time to experiment with your computer system before going on to the more advanced material. Try running the programs from this chapter, as well as some of your own design. Let's get started.

Data Movement

Moving data between registers and between registers and memory is a fundamental requirement of all programs. Many microprocessors provide a variety of machine instructions to perform these operations. The 8086/8088 is no exception. However, in order to make the programmer's job easier, one instruction mnemonic, MOV, is used for all the actual machine instructions that may be needed. The assembler determines which machine instruction is needed by the operands used with the MOV instruction. This means that we can move a constant into a register, a variable into a register, or a register into a register without having to remember different mnemonics for all these instructions.

The general form of the MOV instruction is:

[label] MOV   destination,source   [;comment]

The MOV instruction takes the value of the source operand and places a copy of it into the destination operand. The source operand is not changed.

The destination operand may be a register or a variable, but not a constant. The source operand may be a register, variable, or constant. A number of other instructions have source and destination operands. Always remember that the direction of the data flow is from the right operand to the left operand. You may have used an assembly language for another computer that had things reversed. Be careful when you start programming the 8086/8088 so you don't make a mistake.

Let's assume that the AX and BX registers contain the following values:

AX	BX
1234H	5566H

If we now execute the following instruction:

    MOV   AX,BX

the AX and BX registers would contain the following values after execution:

AX	BX
5566H	5566H

Notice that the previous value in the AX register has been lost and that the new value is identical to the BX register. Also note that the contents of the BX register remain unchanged.

There are a few combinations of source and destination operands that are not allowed by the 8086/8088. We cannot move data from one memory location to another with a single MOV instruction.

    MOV   VAR1,VAR2

is not a legal instruction. We must also be careful that the size of the source operand in bytes matches the size of the destination operand in bytes. We cannot move data from an 8-bit register to or from a 16-bit register. The same rule holds true for memory variables. The following are not legal instructions, and the assembler would tell you so:

    MOV   AH,BX
    MOV   DL,COUNT   ;COUNT IS A 16-BIT VARIABLE

If you must perform a move between two data elements of different lengths, there are techniques that can be used. We will discuss them as we go along. Although it makes no sense, you may write a MOV instruction that tries to store a register or variable into a constant. This is not permitted, but if you forget the order of the source and destination operands, it may come out this way:

    MOV   100,AX

This is not legal.

SELF-CHECK

1) Write an instruction to move the contents of CL to AH.   *MOV AH, CL*
2) Write an instruction to move AX to memory variable SAMPLES.   *MOV SAMPLES, AX*
3) Write an instruction to load register DX with the constant 2526.   *MOV DX, 2526*
4) Is MOV AL, 500H a legal instruction?   *No*

1) MOV AH, CL

2) MOV SAMPLES, AX

3) MOV DX, 2526

4) No, AL is a single-byte register, and the constant is too large.

Quite often a programmer wants to swap the contents of two registers, two memory variables, or between a register and a memory variable. The 8086/8088 provides a special instruction to perform this operation. Before we look at this instruction, let's see how we would program an operation, using only the MOV instruction, to swap the contents of the AX and BX registers. At first a programmer may be tempted to write:

```
MOV    AX,BX
MOV    BX,AX
```

Unfortunately, these two instructions do not accomplish the desired result. The first MOV instruction has destroyed the contents of the AX register, the value that must be placed in the BX register by the second MOV. This second move will erroneously result in the BX register's value not being changed. To perform the swap correctly, we need a temporary storage location. This can be a register or a memory variable. We can write:

```
MOV    CX,AX
MOV    AX,BX
MOV    BX,CX
```

and perform the swap correctly. However, we have used the CX register as a temporary storage location, and we may not wish to destroy its contents either. The use of a memory variable frees the registers but will cause the instructions to execute at a slower speed.

The 8086/8088 XCHG instruction is our salvation. We can swap between registers or between memory and a register, but not between two memory variables. If a swap is performed between a register and memory, the memory variable *must* be the destination operand. We can write the above program as:

```
XCHG   AX,BX
```

If we would like to swap between a memory variable, MYDATA, and the DX register, we must write:

XCHG   MYDATA,DX

Of course, we can't swap two constants or a constant and anything else.

---

1) Write an instruction to swap the high- and low-order bytes of the CX register.   XCHG   CH, CL
2) Write an instruction to swap the memory location MEMC with the AH register.   XCHG   MEMC, AH

1) XCHG CH, CL or XCHG CL, CH

2) XCHG MEMC, AH

Addition and Subtraction

While moving values from one register to another is an important part of assembly language programming, arithmetic operations, such as addition and subtraction, will allow you to start writing programs that actually perform meaningful tasks. The general form of both the add and subtract instructions is:

```
[label] ADD   destination,source   [;comment]
[label] SUB   destination,source   [;comment]
```

The ADD instruction forms the sum of the source and destination operands, which may be words or bytes, and replaces the destination operand with this sum. Both operands may be signed or unsigned numbers. SUB works like ADD, except that the source operand is subtracted from the destination operand. Once again, the result replaces the destination operand. The source operand may be a register, a memory variable, or a constant. The destination operand may be a register or a memory variable. Like the MOV instruction, source and destination operands cannot both be memory variables. The following are all valid ADD and SUB instructions:

```
ADD   AL,AH
SUB   BX,12
ADD   COUNT,1234H
```

As we mentioned when we discussed the MOV instruction, the size, in bytes, of the source and destination operands must be the same. When a constant is used, it must be capable of being represented by the number of bytes of the destination operand. If a 2-byte (word) constant is specified, it cannot be used with MOV, ADD, or SUB instructions in which the destination operand is only a single-byte register or variable. However, if a 1-byte constant is used with a 2-byte destination, the assembler is able to generate the proper machine instruction. The 8086/8088 machine language includes a mechanism in which 8-bit values are automatically sign-extended to 16 bits when needed. The constant still takes up only 8 bits, but it is used as a proper signed 16-bit value. The following instruction is not legal and would be flagged as an error by the assembler:

ADD   AL,BX

The source and destination operands can be the same.

ADD   AL,AL

results in the AL register being doubled.

The 8086/8088 does not have a *clear* instruction. Several methods can be used to clear, or zero, the contents of a register.

SUB   BX,BX

will clear the BX register. We can also use a MOV instruction.

MOV   BX,0000H

There are other clever ways to clear a register that you will discover when additional instructions are presented.

SELF-CHECK

1) Write the instruction to add AH and AL, with the result in AL.   *ADD AL,AH.*
2) Write the instruction to add the constant 5 to register BX.   *ADD BX,5*
3) Write the instructions to add variables N1 and N2. The results should be in register AX.   *SUB AX,AX*
   ADD AX,N1
   ADD AX,N2

1)   ADD AL, AH

2)   ADD BX, 5

3)   MOV AX, N1
     ADD AX, N2

Input and Output

While we can write many programs that do not require data to be entered by the user, we certainly do not want to limit ourselves in this way. We could write programs that manipulate data included in the assembly language source itself. This would be of limited use if this data required frequent modification. Each time we wished to run the program with different data, we would have to edit the source program, then reassemble it. This is time-consuming and would be an unreasonable requirement for many users. What we seek is the ability to obtain data entered from the user's terminal or keyboard at the time the program is executed.

Similarly, we normally require a method for obtaining output from the program during or after its execution. Unless we have some way of displaying the program output on a terminal or a printer, we can only determine a program's action by looking at the contents of variables or registers that have changed during the program's execution. This may be possible with programmer utilities, such as a debugger, but it is certainly not the best way to start programming in assembly language.

Unfortunately, input and output are always dependent on the particular computer you are using. Not all computer systems using the 8086/8088 processor are equipped with the same input/output devices. Some systems have a video display; others may have a typewriterlike terminal. Normally, some degree of hardware independence is provided by the operating system you are using, but here again we will not all be using the same operating system. Some readers may be using CP/M; others may be using MS DOS or one of many other operating systems now on the market.

So that we can start to write programs without worrying about the system-dependent details, we will use a set of input/output procedures whose inner workings will be different for different operating systems. These procedures will assume a standard ASCII terminal or display. Since the interface is through your operating system, the details of your particular hardware are taken care of automatically. It doesn't matter whether you have a video display or a printing terminal. Appendix B gives the actual source statements for these procedures, written for the CP/M and MS DOS (PC DOS) operating systems. While this appendix does not cover every operating system in use, its data will probably accommodate the majority of readers.

Many programs involve inputting one or more decimal numbers from the terminal keyboard and outputting one or more decimal numbers to the terminal. We also need to input and output ASCII characters. Let us start by introducing some useful procedures to perform these tasks. A *procedure*, or subroutine, is a portion of a program that can be referenced, or called, from many different places within the program without repeating the instructions each time the procedure is used. Here they are. Read their descriptions carefully so that you will understand their use.

1. INDEC. Input an unsigned decimal number from the keyboard. The number is entered as one or more decimal digits terminated by a character other than 0 to 9. This terminating character may be a carriage return (RETURN key on most keyboards). The number must be representable by two bytes and must therefore be between 0 and 65,535. The number is placed in the AX register.
2. OUTDEC. Output an unsigned decimal number to the terminal. The number is taken from the AX register. It is output without a terminating carriage return and line feed (doesn't advance to the next line).
3. NEWLINE. Terminate the present output line and output the carriage return and line feed characters to advance to the start of the next line.
4. GETC. Input a single character from the keyboard. The ASCII value of the character is returned in the AL register.
5. PUTC. Output a single character to the terminal. The character is taken from the AL register.

In order to use these procedures within your program, a special instruction, CALL, is provided in the 8086/8088 instruction set. The exact operation of this instruction, and procedures in general, will be discussed in Chapter 8. The mnemonic CALL is followed by the identifier that represents the procedure's name. For now, assume that when you use the CALL instruction, the program performs the operations specified by the procedure that is called, and your program continues to the next instruction. The following program excerpt will obtain two numbers from your keyboard, add them together, then output the result to your terminal:

```
CALL   INDEC
CALL   NEWLINE
MOV    BX,AX
CALL   INDEC
CALL   NEWLINE
ADD    AX,BX
CALL   OUTDEC
CALL   NEWLINE
```

Notice that the third instruction is used to save the contents of the AX register so that the second CALL instruction to INDEC does not destroy the first number to be added. Other than the AX register that is used with the INDEC procedure, the input/output procedures given above do not destroy the contents of any of the 8086/8088 registers. The CALLs to NEWLINE ensure that we advance to the beginning of a new line after each number is input and after the result is output. A call to NEWLINE is required even if you terminate the number you enter with a carriage return. A line feed must be output to advance to the beginning of the next line. The carriage return will only position you at the beginning of the current line.

SELF-CHECK

1) Write the instructions to obtain an input value, add 100, and output the result.
2) Write the instructions to output the constant 1234H.
3) Write the instructions to obtain an input character and repeat it on output.

```
1) CALL   INDEC
   CALL   NEWLINE
   ADD    AX, 100
   CALL   OUTDEC
   CALL   NEWLINE

2) MOV    AX, 1234H
   CALL   OUTDEC
   CALL   NEWLINE

3) CALL   GETC
   CALL   PUTC
   CALL   NEWLINE
```

The Program Shell

In order to write a complete program, certain assembler directives and standard code sequences are needed for each different assembler and operating system. So that we don't have to depend on one particular assembler or operating system, we will not include this program code for each program presented. The *program shell* will enclose each program. Appendix C shows appropriate program shells for CP/M and MS DOS. It is important to note that the shell contains a code and a data segment. Unless it is obvious, we will indicate the code and data segments of future programs with an appropriate comment line. Be sure to place the code and data segments in their proper places in the program shell. Normally, instructions go in the code segment; variables go in the data segment.

You should also note that the code segment is terminated by an appropriate mechanism to return control to your operating system. The 8086/8088 has a halt instruction (HLT), but if this instruction is used to terminate your program, the microprocessor will literally halt, and you will have to reboot (start from scratch) your operating system. It is much better to return control so that you can continue to issue system commands.

To actually start to write programs using the input/output procedures presented in the previous section, the procedures must be included with your program and the shell. If you require one or more of these procedures in your program, copy the appropriate source statements. Place these statements immediately after the return to the operating system. The correct position is indicated in the shell programs. You will have to consult your system documentation to adapt these procedures for other operating systems and/or assemblers.

Looping

With the instructions you have learned so far, it is possible to write a few simple programs that perform addition and subtraction of a limited number of values. For example, if we want to form the sum of twenty numbers entered from your terminal, it would take twenty lines of assembler source code to obtain these values. An additional twenty ADD instructions would be required as well. If we wished to add a larger number of values, we would soon tire of all the typing needed to produce the source program. We must also consider that each assembly language instruction will take one or more bytes of memory space when it is translated into machine language. Quite often we must try to write a small program, as well as an efficient one.

The solution to this problem is the use of a *program loop*. There are many ways to write a program loop for the 8086/8088 microprocessor. The simplest is the infinite loop program loop. It may seem of no value to write an infinite loop, and if there is a method by which we can escape this loop, it will often be useful. We might like a program that repeats itself over and over again for an arbitrary number of input data values, eliminating the need for the user to reinvoke the program for each new value. We will discuss methods of escaping from an infinite loop in the next chapter. For now, let us see how we can write one.

Execution normally passes from one instruction to the next. This is known as sequential execution. The 8086/8088 provides a special instruction for altering the normal sequential program flow. The jump instruction (JMP) allows transfer of control to any instruction that has a label. The following is a simple infinite loop:

```
OVER:   .
        .
        .
        .
        JMP  OVER
```

Any number of instructions can be contained within the loop. We can write a simple program that will obtain a number from the terminal, double it, then output the result. These steps are then repeated over and over.

```
;
;INPUT A VALUE FROM THE TERMINAL, DOUBLE,
;AND THEN OUTPUT THE RESULT
;
NEXT:   CALL   INDEC    ;OBTAIN AN INPUT VALUE
        CALL   NEWLINE
        ADD    AX,AX     ;DOUBLE THE VALUE
        CALL   OUTDEC   ;OUTPUT THE NUMBER
        CALL   NEWLINE
        JMP    NEXT
```

If you decide to actually run this program, you may have to stop your computer manually and reboot your operating system. The exact procedures to follow depend on your particular computer, and you should consult your owner's manual for the details. CP/M and MS-DOS allow you to abort a program, then return to the operating system by typing a Control C. This is the character C typed while holding down the key labeled CTRL.

SELF-CHECK

1) Write an infinite loop that will output the integers starting with zero.
2) Write an infinite loop that outputs the word HELP over and over.

=====

```
1)            MOV    AX, 0
       NEXT:  CALL   OUTDEC
              CALL   NEWLINE
              ADD    AX, 1
              JMP    NEXT
```

(handwritten:)
```
       MOV   AX, 0
       CALL  OUTDEC
loop   CALL  NEWLINE
       ADD   AX, 1
       CALL  OUTDEC
       JMP   LOOP
```

```
2) NEXT:    MOV    AL, 72 ;H
            CALL   PUTC
            MOV    AL, 69 ;E
            CALL   PUTC
            MOV    AL, 76 ;L
            CALL   PUTC
            MOV    AL, 80 ;P
            CALL   PUTC
            CALL   NEWLINE
            JMP    NEXT
```

Another frequently used loop is the counting loop. This loop repeats a number of instructions a fixed number of times. Unlike many microprocessors, the 8086/8088 provides a single instruction to perform a counting loop. In fact, it has the appropriate mnemonic, LOOP, that works like a JMP instruction, except that it uses the value contained in the CX register as a loop counter. It does this by first subtracting one from the current value in CX, then checking to see if the result is equal to zero. If the updated value contained in the CX register is not equal to zero, then the LOOP instruction performs like a JMP to the label specified as the operand. If the new value of CX is zero, then the next sequential instruction is executed.

In order to use the LOOP instruction, we must first set up the CX register with the *total* number of times we wish to go through the loop instructions. These are the instructions between the label of the LOOP and the LOOP instruction itself. The instructions will always be executed at least once, even if we initialize CX with zero. In fact, initializing CX to zero results in repeating the loop the maximum number of times, 65,536, to be exact. As a simple example, let's say we want to output twenty blank lines. We could call the NEWLINE procedure twenty times by writing twenty lines of assembler source, or we could write the following three lines:

```
            MOV    CX,20
   NEXT:    CALL   NEWLINE
            LOOP   NEXT
```

SELF-CHECK

1) Write a counting loop to output the digits 0 through 9.
2) Write a counting loop that sums the digits 1 through 9 and outputs the result.

```
1)          MOV    AL, 48      ;ASCII CODE FOR ZERO
            MOV    CX, 10
   NEXT:    CALL   PUTC
            CALL   NEWLINE
            ADD    AL, 1       ;NEXT DIGIT
            LOOP   NEXT
```

```
2)            MOV    AX, 0
              MOV    BX, 1
              MOV    CX, 9
    NEXT:     ADD    AX, BX
              ADD    BX, 1
              LOOP   NEXT
              CALL   OUTDEC
              CALL   NEWLINE
```

We must be careful not to modify the contents of the CX register within the program loop. If we were to change CX, it would no longer represent the loop count, and the result would not be what you desired. If you must use the CX register within the loop, you must save and restore it. You could move the contents to another register or to a variable. Here's how to do it with a variable:

```
;CODE SEGMENT
              .
              .
              .
              MOV    CX,100
    NEXT:     MOV    SAVECX,CX
              .
              .
              .
              .
              MOV    CX,SAVECX
              LOOP   NEXT
              .
              .
              .
;DATA SEGMENT
SAVECX   DW       0
```

You have probably noticed that we have a data segment present in this program. Up to this point we have not mentioned how to provide for memory variables. Each variable that you wish to use in your program must be *declared* in the data segment if it is to be referenced in the code segment. Remember to place the source statements for the code and data segments in proper positions in the program shell.

The mnemonic DW in the operation field is not actually an 8086/8088 instruction. It is an assembler directive, instructing the assembler to define a word in memory with the initial value zero. In this case, the initial value is not important, but we often want variables to be initilized to predetermined values. Other directives that can be used to define variables will be discussed in Chapter 6.

One restriction with the LOOP instruction is not found with the JMP instruction. With the JMP instruction, we can transfer control to any distant label; in other words, we can have loops of arbitrary size. Unfortunately, the

LOOP instruction (and many others, you will discover) allows transfer of control over only a limited distance. This distance is approximately plus or minus 128 bytes from the position of the LOOP instruction itself. We can't represent this distance as a fixed number of instructions because the number of bytes per instruction varies with the particular instruction. Fortunately, the assembler will tell us if we can't fit all the instructions into the loop. There are several methods we can use to get around the problem.

Putting It All Together

Figure 7 shows a complete program that will output a table of the powers of two from 2^1 to 2^{15}. As you learned in Chapter 1, 2^{15} is the largest power of two that we can represent with a 16-bit unsigned number. The program is written as one counting loop. The CX register is initialized to 15, the number of powers we wish to output. MLOOP is the label referenced by the LOOP instruction, the last instruction of the program prior to the return to the operating system. We also declared two variables, EXP and POWER, to represent the current exponent and the actual power of two for the value of EXP. These two variables are initialized prior to entering the main loop. Each successive power is computed by doubling the previous power with the ADD AX,AX instruction. Since the AX register is used for several functions, POWER and EXP are updated after their new values are computed.

```
;THE CODE SEGMENT
            MOV    CX,15        ;SET UP MAIN LOOP COUNT
            MOV    EXP,1        ;INITIALIZE EXPONENT
            MOV    POWER,2      ;    AND POWER
MLOOP:      MOV    AX,EXP       ;GET EXPONENT
            CALL   OUTDEC       ;OUTPUT EXPONENT
            ADD    AX,1         ;INCREMENT
            MOV    EXP,AX       ;    AND SAVE
            MOV    AL,20H       ;OUTPUT A SPACE
            CALL   PUTC
            MOV    AX,POWER     ;GET POWER OF TWO
            CALL   OUTDEC       ;OUTPUT VALUE
            ADD    AX,AX        ;DOUBLE FOR NEXT TIME
            MOV    POWER,AX     ;    AND SAVE
            CALL   NEWLINE      ;GO TO NEXT LINE
            LOOP   MLOOP        ;BACK FOR MORE
;
;THE DATA SEGMENT
EXP         DW     0
POWER       DW     0
;
```

Figure 7. Program to output powers of two.

To format the output lines, insert a space after outputting the exponent, then advance to the next line after outputting the power. The ASCII character value for the space character is 20 in hexadecimal. The standard procedure, PUTC, is called with this value in the AL register. The output from this program should look like this:

```
1 2
2 4
3 8
4 16
5 32
6 64
7 128
8 256
9 512
10 1024
11 2048
12 4096
13 8192
14 16384
15 32768
```

SELF-TEST

1) How does the assembler know which of the many MOV instructions to generate?
2) Which is correct?
   MOV   destination,source
   or
   MOV   source,destination
3) Write a move instruction to move the SI register to the AX register.
4) Write the instruction or instructions necessary to move the contents of word variable XYZ to variable COPYXYZ.
5) Write the instruction to swap the BX and BP registers.
6) Is ADD BX,CL a legal instruction? If not, why not?
7) Write the instructions necessary to evaluate AX−BX+CX+100, with the result placed in variable RESULT.
8) Why have input/output procedures been provided?
9) Write the instructions necessary to input a value, double it, subtract 1, and output the result.
10) Write the instructions necessary to output the letter A 1000 times, with 10 per line.

1) By the types of the operands. For example, constants, registers, or variables.
2) MOV   destination,source
3) MOV   AX, SI

```
4) MOV   AX, XYZ
   MOV   COPYXYZ, AX
```

Remember that we cannot move a memory variable into another memory variable with a single MOV instruction.

```
5) XCHG  BP, BX
```
or
```
   XCHG  BX, BP
```

6) This instruction is not legal. The source and destination operands must be the same size.

```
7) SUB   AX, BX
   ADD   BX, CX
   ADD   BX, 100
   MOV   RESULT, BX
```

8) Because input/output is machine- and operating system-dependent, and it is best to perform these operations by procedures that can be isolated from the rest of the program.

```
9)         CALL   INDEC
           CALL   NEWLINE
           ADD    AX, AX
           SUB    AX, 1
           CALL   OUTDEC
           CALL   NEWLINE
```

```
10)        MOV    AL, 'A'
           MOV    CX, 100
   OUTL:   MOV    BX, CX
           MOV    CX, 10
   INL:    CALL   PUTC
           LOOP   INL
           CALL   NEWLINE
           MOV    CX, BX
           LOOP   OUTL
```

CHAPTER 5

Conditional and Arithmetic Instructions

In Chapter 4 you learned a small number of 8086/8088 instructions, enough to write some very simple programs. I hope that you have taken the time to actually run some of the programs presented in the chapter, as well as a few programs of your own design. Nothing will give you more confidence in successfully mastering assembly language programming than the joy you experience when a program actually performs as it should. By now you should have become familiar with your own computer's procedures for editing, assembling, and executing assembly language programs. If you are having trouble, then you should carefully review your computer system's manuals before going on with this chapter.

The remainder of this book is designed to expand your vocabulary of 8086/8088 instructions. Rather than present *all* the remaining instructions at one time, we will present groups of instructions and specific examples of their use. You should not attempt to learn all of the 8086/8088 instructions before practicing with each group. Take the time to experiment with the instructions presented in each chapter. Don't limit yourself to the exercises. Be creative.

In this chapter you will learn the powerful set of conditional instructions. These allow the control flow of your program to vary, depending on the results of instructions such as the arithmetic instructions you have already learned, as well as several others. Crucial to understanding the conditional instructions is a thorough knowledge of certain bits in the flag register and how these bits are affected by arithmetic instructions.

Arithmetic and the Flag Register

As you learned in Chapter 2, the 8086/8088 has a special register known as the flag register. This register is not used in the same way as the other registers. We don't treat the contents of the flag register as a numeric quantity. Instead, we indirectly use the values of *individual* bits in the flag register.

Each of these special bits has a specific meaning when set or reset. If a bit is set, it has a value of binary one. If it is reset, it has a value of binary zero. The flag register is a 16-bit register, but not all of the 16 bits are used. The flag register is organized as follows:

Flag Register

15   0

			OF	DF	IF	TF	SF	ZF		AF		PF	CF

OF	Overflow Flag
DF	Direction Flag
IF	Interrupt Flag
TF	Trap Flag
SF	Sign Flag
ZF	Zero Flag
AF	Auxiliary Carry Flag
PF	Parity Flag
CF	Carry Flag

SELF-CHECK

1) Is the flag register used in the same way as other registers?
2) How many bits are in the flag register?
3) How many are actually used?
4) If a bit in the flag register is set, does it have a value of binary one or zero?

1) No.
2) 16
3) 9
4) One.

After the execution of an 8086/8088 instruction, some of the flags may be affected. Not all instructions affect the flags. The majority of flag usage is related to arithmetic operations, such as addition, subtraction, and the comparison of two numeric quantities. Since this chapter will be concerned with arithmetic operations, we will examine only the flags that are used with these instructions. We will cover the remaining flags as they are needed.

In Chapter 1 we discussed the representation of numbers in two's complement binary. Remember that numbers can be interpreted as signed or unsigned, depending on the interpretation of the most significant bit. We refer to this bit as the sign bit for signed numbers. Often we will want to treat a number as a positive value only. By allowing the use of the most significant bit as a normal bit of the number, and not as a sign, we can double the magnitude of the numbers we can represent. The ADD and SUB instructions operate identically for both signed and unsigned numbers. The interpretation is up to the programmer. However, through the use of particular flags in the flag register, we can test the outcome of arithmetic operations for both signed *and* unsigned numbers.

SELF-CHECK

1) Are *all* the flags affected by *all* instructions?
2) Do the ADD and SUB instructions treat signed and unsigned numbers differently?
3) Is the sign bit the high- or low-order bit?

1) No, not all instructions affect the flags, and not all the flags are affected by those instructions that do affect the flags.
2) No, the interpretation is up to the programmer.
3) High-order bit.

The Carry Flag

One of the most important checks we must make on an arithmetic operation is whether or not the result has exceeded the size of the destination register. For example, if we add the following unsigned 8-bit binary numbers, we get a result that will not fit into an 8-bit destination (register or memory byte).

```
  11101001
+ 10110111
 110100000
```

The carry of a bit from the most significant (high-order) bit position has no place to go. Actually, this event causes the carry flag (CF) to be set. If there had been no carry, then the carry flag would be reset.

When we want to determine whether the result of an unsigned addition is valid, we must somehow test the setting of the carry flag. Fortunately, the 8086/8088 provides a group of instructions that allow the testing of each of the flags individually and a number of them in combination. These instructions all have the form of a conditional jump. A conditional jump is similar to a JMP instruction, except that the jump is not taken unless the particular condition is true. The condition corresponds to the value or values of one or more of the flags. If the jump is not taken, then the next sequential instruction is executed. The jump on carry instruction (JC) provides a conditional jump based on the setting of the carry flag. If the carry flag is set (binary one), then the jump is taken. The following program illustrates the use of the JC instruction to validate the result of an unsigned addition.

```
         MOV   AX,NUM1
         ADD   AX,NUM2
         JC    INVALID
                  .            ;RESULT IS OK
                  .
                  .
INVALID:          .            ;RESULT EXCEEDS REGISTER SIZE
                  .
                  .
```

The label used with the JC instruction, and with *all* the conditional jumps, must be to a location that is approximately plus or minus 128 bytes of the location of the instruction itself. As we mentioned in Chapter 5, this restriction is also present with the LOOP instruction. Since it is usually not possible to easily tell how many instructions will represent 128 bytes, it is best to let the assembler do the work for you. But let's suppose that you must perform a conditional jump to a location greater than plus or minus 128 bytes. What can you do to get around this problem? One simple solution is to perform the conditional jump to a JMP instruction that is close to the conditional jump, then have the JMP instruction actually jump to the target label. Here's how we do it:

```
                  .
                  .
                  .
         JC    CLOSE        ─────────────────┐
                  .                          │
                  .              < 128 BYTES │
                  .                          │
CLOSE:   JMP   FARWAY       ──────────────┐  │
                  .                       │  │
                  .            > 128 BYTES│  │
                  .                       │  │
                  .                       │  │
FARWAY:           .         ──────────────┘──┘
                  .
```

We can also do this:

```
                  .
                  .
                  .
         JC    CLOSE
         JMP   NEXT
CLOSE:   JMP   FARWAY
NEXT:             .
                  .
                  .
```

The second approach has the advantage that we know the JMP is close enough, and we have a definite place for it to go without interfering with other instructions. We can make the solution to this problem even simpler if we reverse the condition upon which we jump. In other words, if we could perform a conditional jump when the carry flag was *not* set, rather than set, then we could use the conditional jump to go to the next sequential instruction in the program. We are in luck! The 8086/8088 provides complementary instructions for all conditional jumps. We can always find an appropriate conditional jump that jumps when the condition we wish to test is *not* true. In the case of the JC instruction, the JNC (jump on no carry) is the one to use. Our program can now be written:

```
            .
            .
        JNC   NEXT
        JMP   FARWAY
NEXT:     .
          .
```

Several instructions are provided to manipulate the carry flag explicitly. These instructions are:

STC	Set carry flag
CLC	Clear carry flag
CMC	Complement carry flag

These instructions have no operands. STC will set the carry flag to one. CLC clears the carry flag by setting it to zero. The CMC instruction flips the carry flag. In other words, if it had been a zero, it is set to one, and vice versa.

The Overflow Flag

What if we are adding signed numbers? A carry out of the high-order bit is not necessarily indicative of a result that is too large. Adding two negative numbers will result in the carry flag's being set.

```
  11111110   -2
+ 11111111   -1
  111111101  -3
```

We detect a result that is too large if the sign bit (the most significant bit) changes when we don't want it to. This condition is known as *overflow*. The overflow flag (OF) is set or reset depending on the occurrence of the overflow condition. OF is affected by all arithmetic instructions, regardless of whether we are treating the operands as signed or unsigned numbers. The 8086/8088 instructions don't know the difference. We must use either CF or OF, respectively, for signed or unsigned arithmetic. The jump on overflow (JO) and jump on no overflow (JNO) instructions are provided for signed arithmetic.

Subtraction results in similar effects on CF and OF. If an unsigned subtraction results in a borrow into the most significant bit position, then the carry flag is set. Since an unsigned subtraction cannot result in a negative value, this is an error. The overflow flag is set for subtractions as well. If we subtract a positive number from a negative number and the result is a negative number that is too large, OF will be set. Overflow can also result from subtracting a negative number from a positive number. If the positive result is too large, OF will be set.

Zero and Sign Flags

In addition to determining whether the result of an arithmetic operation has exceeded the size capacity of the destination register, a programmer may also want to know whether the result is positive, negative, or zero. The zero flag (ZF) and the sign flag (SF) are provided for these purposes. The zero flag is set if the numerical result is zero. This means that all bits of the result are zero. The jump on zero (JZ) and jump on not zero (JNZ) instructions will conditionally jump depending on the value of ZF.

One example of the use of ZF is to show the equivalent program code for the LOOP instruction:

```
        MOV   CX,COUNT
NEXT:    .
         .
         .
        SUB   CX,1
        JNZ   NEXT
         .
         .
```

We can also use a zero value as a signal to exit an indefinite loop. The following program adds input values until a zero is entered, then outputs the result.

```
        MOV   BX,0       ;INITIALIZE THE SUM
MORE:   CALL  INDEC      ;GET NEXT INPUT VALUE
        CALL  NEWLINE
        ADD   AX,0       ;TO SET/RESET THE ZERO FLAG
        JZ    DONE       ;DONE IF ZERO
        ADD   BX,AX      ;ADD IT UP
        JMP   MORE       ;BACK FOR MORE
DONE:   MOV   AX,BX      ;GET INTO THE PROPER REG
        CALL  OUTDEC     ;OUTPUT THE RESULT
        CALL  NEWLINE
```

The ADD instruction on the fourth line does not change the value of the data; it merely serves to ensure that the zero flag is set or reset properly. There are many ways to do this besides the ADD instruction. Any instruction that sets/resets ZF and does not change the value of the data will work. For example, we could just as well subtract a zero value.

We may also want to determine whether an arithmetic operation results in a positive or negative value. The sign bit will be set to a binary one for all negative numbers. Note that zero is always a positive number in two's complement. The sign flag is set to the same value as the sign bit of the result of the operation. The jump on sign (JS) and jump on not sign (JNS) instructions will test for negative and positive numbers respectively. Be careful not to try using the mnemonic JP for jump on positive. This mnemonic is actually the jump on parity instruction. It will not work as you expect.

SELF-CHECK

1) What flag is used to detect overflow of unsigned arithmetic operations?
2) What flag is used to detect overflow of signed arithmetic operations?
3) Is there a limit as to how far away the label of a conditional jump may be?
4) What instructions manipulate the carry flag directly?
5) What flag determines whether the result of an arithmetic operation is zero?
6) What flag determines whether the result of an arithmetic operation is positive or negative?

========

1) The carry flag, CF.
2) The overflow flag, OF.
3) Yes, approximately plus or minus 128 bytes.
4) Set carry, STC; clear carry, CLC; complement carry, CMC.
5) The zero flag, ZF.
6) The sign flag, SF.

Comparisons

An essential task that we must be able to perform in any programming language is the comparison of two numbers, or of any data items being represented by numerical values. ASCII characters are an example of the latter. We could perform a subtraction of the two numbers, then test the flags to determine their relationship. If the two values are equal to each other, the zero flag will be set. We can also test the carry flag, sign flag, etc., to determine other inequalities. The particular flags we must test depend on whether we are comparing signed or unsigned quantities. We must be careful to test for overflow as well, which may result in a requirement to test two or more flags. *NOT NECESSARY*

A disadvantage in performing a subtraction to compare two numbers is the fact that the destination operand will be changed. Since the destination operand must be one of the values to be compared, we will destroy its value. We could, of course, make a copy. The following code will compare two numbers to determine whether or not they are equal to each other.

```
          MOV   AX,NUM1   ;MAKE A COPY OF NUM1
          SUB   AX,25     ;SUBTRACT 25
          JZ    EQUAL
                  .        ;NOT EQUAL
                  .
EQUAL:            .        ;EQUAL
                  .
```

There is a better way to compare numbers. A special compare instruction (CMP) works almost like the SUB instruction, except that the result of the subtraction is not actually saved. In other words, the operands remain unchanged. All the flags that would be set or reset by the SUB instruction are also set or reset by the CMP instruction. Like the ADD and SUB instructions, the destination operand can be a register or a variable, and the source operand can be a register, a variable, or a constant. Both cannot be variables.

The previous example can be rewritten using the CMP instruction.

```
          CMP   NUM1,25
          JE    EQUAL
                  .
                  .
EQUAL:            .
                  .
```

Since we are using the CMP instruction and not an SUB, the value of NUM1 does not have to be copied. You may also note that a jump on equal (JE) instruction has been used, instead of the jump on zero (JZ). Actually, these are identical instructions. The assembler provides two mnemonics for the same instruction. When we are comparing two values, this makes it clearer to the reader of the program that we are really interested in whether or not the two values are equal. A number of other conditional jumps have multiple mnemonics.

In general we will want to compare both signed and unsigned numbers. The standard inequalities all have unique conditional jumps that are used with the CMP instruction. For inequalities other than equal or not equal, it is sometimes difficult to remember which value should be the source and which the destination. The CMP instruction compares the destination with the source. Therefore, if we wish to determine whether AX is less than or equal to BX, we would write

```
CMP   AX,BX
JLE   LABEL
```

The following table shows the conditional jumps for signed numbers.

		Mnemonic
<	JL	Jump on less
<=	JLE	Jump on less or equal
=	JE	Jump on equal
>=	JGE	Jump on greater or equal
>	JG	Jump on greater
not =	JNE	Jump on not equal

When you compare unsigned numbers, you should use the following.

<	JB	Jump on below
<=	JBE	Jump on below or equal
=	JE	Jump on equal
>=	JAE	Jump on above or equal
>	JA	Jump on above
not =	JNE	Jump on not equal

The tests for equal and not equal use the same conditional jumps for both signed and unsigned numbers.

Each of the conditional jumps has a second mnemonic that is the negation of the opposite test. In other words, jump on less is identical to jump on not greater or equal. Therefore, the JNGE mnemonic is an equivalent way of specifying the JL instruction. The following table lists all the equivalent mnemonics for the conditional jumps.

JB/JNAE/JC	JL/JNGE
JBE/JNA	JLE/JNG
JE/JZ	JNE/JNZ
JAE/JNB/JNC	JG/JNLE
JA/JNBE	JGE/JNL

The following program finds the largest unsigned number from an arbitrary number of input values. Entering a zero value terminates input and outputs the result.

```
        MOV    BX,0       ;INITIALIZE THE LARGEST VALUE
MORE:   CALL   INDEC      ;GET NEXT INPUT VALUE
        CALL   NEWLINE
        CMP    AX,0       ;EXIT VALUE?
        JE     DONE       ;YES
        CMP    AX,BX      ;IS IT > LARGEST?
        JBE    MORE       ;NO
        MOV    BX,AX      ;YES, SAVE AS NEW LARGEST
        JMP    MORE       ;BACK FOR MORE
DONE:   MOV    AX,BX      ;GET INTO THE PROPER REG
        CALL   OUTDEC     ;OUTPUT THE RESULT
        CALL   NEWLINE
```

Two CMP instructions are used. The first CMP tests for the zero terminating value. The second determines whether a new input value is larger than the largest value encountered so far. It is important to remember to initialize this value to something meaningful. In this case, a zero value is smaller than any value we will encounter.

One more conditional jump instruction remains, the jump on CX zero (JCXZ). This instruction merely tests the value of register CX and jumps if it is zero. The instruction JCXZ SOMEPLACE is equivalent to the following instructions:

```
CMP    CX, 0
JZ     SOMEPLACE
```

SELF-CHECK

1) What is the difference between the CMP instruction and the SUB instruction? *SUB Changes value of Destination*
2) Is there a difference between the JZ and JE instructions? *No*
3) Write the instructions necessary to jump to label STOP if the BL register is equal to 100.

(CMP BL,100
JZ Stop)

4) Write the instructions to jump to label BIGER if register BX is larger than variable LIMIT. Assume unsigned values.

(Comp BX, Limit
JA BIGER)

5) Write the alternative mnemonics for the following instructions:

```
JB    JAE     JNAE    JNB
JL    JNE     JNGE    JNZ
```

---

1) The SUB instruction stores the result of the subtraction in the destination; the CMP performs the same subtraction but does not store the result. The effect on the flags is identical for both instructions.
2) No, they are two different mnemonics for the same instruction.
3) ```
CMP   BL, 100
JE   STOP
```
4) ```
CMP    BX, LIMIT
JA     BIGER
```
5) ```
JB/JNAE/JC   JAE/JNB/JNC
JL/JNGE   JNE/JNZ
```

---

## Increment and Decrement Instructions

Many programs require adding or subtracting the constant, one, from a register or variable. We can naturally use the ADD or SUB instruction to perform this operation. ADD AX,1 increments the value in the AX register. SUB VAR55,1 decrements variable VAR55. The 8086/8088 instruction set offers a better way to increment or decrement an unsigned number. It provides the decrement (DEC) and increment (INC) instructions to increment or decrement an unsigned byte or word in a register or variable. All arithmetic flags are updated, with the exception of the carry flag. This is important to remember if you are attempting to detect overflow while incrementing or decrementing an unsigned number. Since we are always incrementing or decrementing by one, we can detect overflow by checking for a particular value following the increment or decrement instruction. Overflow while incrementing occurs when the value changes from the largest unsigned
```

number, 255 for a byte and 65,535 for a word, to a zero. We can use the jump on zero (JZ) conditional instruction to detect this.

```
INC   BX          ;DO UNSIGNED INCREMENT
JZ    OVRFLOW     ;CHECK FOR OVERFLOW
```

If we are decrementing an unsigned number, we are in trouble if we try to decrement a zero value. This actually gives us a negative one (−1). But since unsigned numbers are always treated as positive, the actual value corresponds to the largest unsigned numbers. We can naturally perform an explicit comparison for these values and use a jump on equal (JE) instruction to detect the overflow. If this is a program requirement, you are probably better off using the SUB instruction and testing the carry flag. If the number we are incrementing or decrementing is a signed number, the overflow flag can be used as it is in normal arithmetic operations. The INC and DEC instructions really don't know the difference between a signed and an unsigned number. This interpretation is always the responsibility of the programmer who chooses appropriate ways to test the validity of an operation.

By now you may be asking yourself why we have an increment and decrement instruction. It is true that the use of INC and DEC saves a small amount of typing of the source program, but this is not the real reason. One minor reason why it is nice to have an increment and decrement instruction is that it makes it clearer to the reader of the program that an increment or decrement by one is taking place, rather than the addition or subtraction of an arbitrary value. However, the most important reason is that, unlike the ADD or SUB instruction, we don't need to provide a source operand. Even the constant one when used with the ADD or SUB instruction must take up one byte of memory. The INC and DEC instructions save this byte by making the constant one implicit in the instruction itself.

The 8086/8088 provides many instructions that can be functionally duplicated by other instructions. When a programmer uses the more appropriate instructions, programs are more readable and take up less space in memory. This is important for large programs, or when there is only a small amount of memory. We will make extensive use of the INC and DEC instructions for a variety of purposes throughout this book.

SELF-TEST

1) What flags were discussed in this chapter?
2) Are all the bits of the flag register used?
3) If we add the following unsigned bytes, will the carry flag be set? The values are in decimal.

    55 and 27
    150 and 110

4) If we add the following signed bytes, will the overflow flag be set? The values are in decimal.

   −100 and +50

   −100 and −50

5) Write the instructions necessary to add the signed values in the AX and BX registers and jump to label OK if there is no overflow.

6) Repeat the above problem for unsigned values.

7) Write the instructions necessary to test whether or not register AX is zero and, if so, jump to label ZERO.

8) Write the instructions necessary to compare variables NUM1 and NUM2. Jump to label EQUAL if they are equal. Jump to label LESS if NUM1 is less than NUM2. Assume signed values.

9) What are the opposite tests for the following:

   JB   JLE   JGE   JA

10) Write the equivalent of the LOOP instruction, using instructions introduced in this chapter.

11) Do the INC and DEC instructions affect the carry flag?

12) Write the equivalent of the INC and DEC instructions, using an ADD or SUB. Are they truly equivalent?

---

1) The carry flag, CF; the overflow flag, OF; the sign flag, SF; the zero flag, ZF.

2) No, only 9 out of 16.

3) 55 and 27 will not result in the carry flag's being set; 150 and 110 will cause an unsigned overflow, and the carry flag will be set.

4) −100 and +50 will not overflow, and the overflow flag will not be set. Even though −100 and −50 do not result in an unsigned overflow, the largest negative number is only −128; therefore the overflow flag will be set.

5) ADD   AX, BX
   JNO   OK

6) ADD   AX, BX
   JNC   OK

7) CMP   AX, 0
   JE   ZERO

8) MOV   AX, NUM1
   CMP   AX, NUM2
   JE   EQUAL
   JL   LESS

9) JB   → JAE
   JLE   → JG
   JGE   → JL
   JA   → JBE

10) DEC   CX
    JCX0   label

11) No.

12) INC op → ADD op, 1
    DEC op → SUB op, 1

They are not truly equivalent because ADD and SUB affect the carry flag; additionally, the number of bytes used by these instructions differs from the bytes used by the INC or DEC.

CHAPTER 6

Assembler Directives

In this chapter you will be introduced to assembler directives, or *pseudo-ops,* as they are also known. An assembler directive provides information to the assembler. The use of assembler directives is similar to forming assembler source statements containing instruction mnemonics. The general format is:

[symbol]   pseudo-op   [operands]   [;comment]

An assembler directive may or may not cause the assembler to generate object bytes to be placed into memory. We can easily differentiate an assembler directive from a machine instruction as there are no duplications of the identifiers. No assembler directive can have the same identifier as a machine instruction.

Data-Defining Directives

In Chapter 4 I mentioned that all variables used in your program must be declared or defined somewhere in your program. When you place a label on an instruction statement, the symbol you have chosen is defined by its association with the memory location of the machine instruction. No such association can be made when a symbol appears *only* as an operand. The data-defining directives are used to declare variables.

Each variable defined has a set of associated attributes. The most important attributes are:

1. The segment containing the variable.
2. The offset within the segment where the variable is found.
3. The type or size of the variable.

The segment attribute associates the appropriate physical segment with the variable so that the proper segment register can be used to access the variable. Most of your variables will be placed in a data segment. The offset within the segment is the position of the variable relative to the start of the segment, always a 16-bit value. The type of variable is associated with its size.

Save Over 62%*

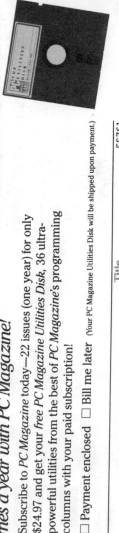

Get in-depth, hands-on product reviews, comprehensive evaluations and special reports to add more power to your IBM/MS DOS standard system *22 times a year with PC Magazine!*

Subscribe to *PC Magazine* today—22 issues (one year) for only $24.97 and get your *free PC Magazine Utilities Disk*, 36 ultra-powerful utilities from the best of *PC Magazine's* programming columns with your paid subscription!

☐ Payment enclosed ☐ Bill me later (Your PC Magazine Utilities Disk will be shipped upon payment.)

Free with your paid subscription!

5S761

Name _____ Title _____

Company _____

Address _____

City/State/Zip _____

Add $15 per year outside USA, US currency only. Please allow up to 60 days for delivery of first issue.
Regular one-year (22 issues) subscription price $34.97.
*Savings based on single copy price of $2.95 per issue.

BUSINESS REPLY MAIL

FIRST CLASS   PERMIT NO. 66   BOULDER, COLORADO

POSTAGE WILL BE PAID BY ADDRESSEE

P.O. Box 2443
Boulder, Colorado 80321

NO POSTAGE
NECESSARY
IF MAILED
IN THE
UNITED STATES

A BYTE variable is one byte long. A WORD variable is two bytes long and a DWORD is four bytes long. Other types may be allowed by some assemblers, but these three are the most useful and are included by all assemblers for the 8086/8088.

The three directives used to define a BYTE, WORD, or DWORD are DB, DW, and DD. All three must have one or more operands. These operands specify the initial values for the variables. If more than one operand is used, they must be separated by commas. The general form of the data-defining directives is:

```
[variable name]  DB   expression [,expression]
[variable name]  DW   expression [,expression]
[variable name]  DD   expression [,expression]
```

The operand expressions must specify a value that can be represented by the appropriate number of bytes. Here are several examples.

```
ABYTE    DB    5
LIST     DB    1,2,3
BIGNUM   DW    65535
NEGVAL   DW    -100
BIGER    DD    9999999
```

It would not be legal to write

```
VAL     DB     300
```

because the maximum unsigned number that can be represented by a single byte is 255.

SELF-CHECK

What are the maximum size signed and unsigned numbers you can use with the following?
1) The DB directive.
2) The DW directive.

	Signed	Unsigned
1)	127 or −128	255
2)	32767 or −32768	65535

Quite often we wish to initialize an array of bytes to an ASCII character string. The DB directive is the only data-defining directive that allows us to use arbitrary length character strings. The statement

```
STRING DB    'HELLO'
```

will initialize a list of consecutive bytes to the ASCII character codes corresponding to HELLO. The character string must be enclosed in single quotes. These quotes do not appear in the data.

Using the DB directive in this way allows us to output messages and other textual information by a simple program loop. We must, however, have some way of knowing the length of the string. We can define constants to represent the length of each character string stored in memory. An alternative approach is to place a special terminating character at the end of the string. Naturally, this character cannot also appear in the middle of the string. Let us say that we use @ (the commercial at) as a terminator. Our program to output this character string would merely have to output each character until it encountered the @. One problem remains. How do we advance through the character string? The symbol we use to define the character string will represent the attributes of only the first character. Fortunately, there is an easy way to do this. The 8086/8088 has a special *addressing mode* that allows us to place the offset attribute of a variable in a register, then use this register to access the variable. Let's show the program first and then discuss it.

```
;
        MOV   BX,OFFSET STRING ;GET OFFSET OF STRING
MORE:   MOV   AL,[BX]          ;GET A CHARACTER
        CMP   AL,'@'           ;IS IT THE TERM CHAR?
        JE    FINI             ;  YES
        CALL  PUTC             ;OUTPUT THE CHARACTER
        INC   BX               ;ADVANCE TO NEXT
                               ;CHAR. POS
        JMP   MORE
FINI:   . . .
;
;THE DATA SEGMENT
;
STRING DB    'THIS IS FUN@'
```

The first MOV instruction places the offset attribute of the variable STRING in the BX register. The special operator, OFFSET, tells the assembler that we want the offset attribute of the particular variable specified. Remember that this is a 16-bit quantity. At first glance, the MOV instruction at the label MORE looks as if it merely copies this 16-bit value into the AL register. If this were so, we would have a problem. Since the AL register is only 8 bits, the value would not fit. However, this is not the action of the MOV instruction. Notice that the BX register designator is enclosed in square brackets. These brackets indicate that instead of using the value contained in the BX register as the source operand, we use this value as the offset into the data segment where the actual operand is found. Since we initialized BX with the offset of STRING, we will get the first byte of the string.

How does the assembler know that it needs to specify a byte rather than a word? The destination operand is a byte operand. This makes it clear that we must have a byte operand as the source. Sometimes it is not clear whether we are to use a byte or a word. In that case there are additional operators that can be used to tell the assembler what we really intend. We will discuss these when we cover the additional addressing modes of the 8086/8088.

The only other instruction to be explained is the INC. This instruction is used to ensure that BX will contain the offset of the next character in the string. Since we are dealing with bytes, we must add one to the value in BX to position ourselves at the next character in the string. When we use the offset of a data element in such a manner, we refer to the offset as a *pointer*. In other words, BX points to the position of the next character.

Sometimes we want to reserve a large block of storage for use as a buffer. We don't really care what the initial contents of the block are. If we use a question mark as the expression value, the assembler will place an indeterminate value in the variable location. We could use as many DB, DW, or DD directives as it would take to reserve this storage. For example, to reserve a buffer of 10 bytes, we could write

```
TENBYTES    DB    ?,?,?,?,?,?,?,?,?,?
```

This gets rather boring if we have to reserve several thousand bytes. There is a better way. It is called a duplicated clause. Any of the operand expressions of a data-defining directive can have the form

```
repeat-count  DUP(expression[,expression])
```

The expressions within the DUP can even be additional DUPs. To reserve 1000 bytes of storage, which is initialized to an indeterminate value, we would write

```
BUFFER  DB  1000 DUP(?)
```

To initialize a block of storage to a repeated ASCII character string, we merely use the character string with a DUP and an appropriate count.

```
STRINGS DB  5 DUP('HELLO')
```

will initialize 25 bytes to the string HELLO repeated five times.

The Digital Research ASM-86 assembler does not allow the use of the DUP clause. Instead, it provides three additional assembler directives, RB, RW, and RS. The general form of all three is:

```
[symbol]  RB    numeric-expression
[symbol]  RW    numeric-expression
[symbol]  RS    numeric-expression
```

RB and RW reserve a block of bytes or words. The number of bytes or words reserved is equal to the value of the numeric expression. RS is just like RB, except that it does not give the BYTE attribute to the optional symbol.

SELF-CHECK
Write the appropriate directive to initialize a block of memory to the following values:

1) 1, 2, 3 repeated 25 times.
2) 5, 5, 5, 6, 6, 6, 6 repeated 10 times.
3) The character string "NOW IS THE TIME"

━━━━━━

1) CONSTS   DB   25 DUP(1,2,3)

2) CONSTS   DB   10 DUP(3 DUP(5), 4 DUP(6))

3) STRNG   DB   'NOW IS THE TIME'

Symbol-Defining Directives

The symbols we use as labels for instructions are defined by their presence in the label field. So are the names we choose for variables we declare with the data-defining directives. Occasionally it is desirable to define symbols of our own choice to represent values not directly associated with the location of an instruction or variable. The EQU directive can be used to assign appropriate attributes to a symbol of your choice. The general form is

    symbol EQU   expression   [;comment]

The expression can be

1. A numerical expression.
2. An address expression.
3. A register.
4. An instruction mnemonic.

Some assemblers allow additional types of expressions, but these are the most common and should be usable with all assemblers.

If the expression is a numerical expression, the symbol can be used as a constant. It is good programming practice to define a symbol with a constant value if that constant is to be used in several places within the program. In that way, should you need to change the constant, you will only have to change the symbol definition. Your program will also be more readable since the symbol name can be used to impart meaning to the constant. Suppose we have a program involving the processing of a number of data elements that may vary from time to time. We can use an EQU directive to set this size at the beginning of the program.

```
ELEMENTS EQU    125               ;NUMBER OF DATA
                                  ;ELEMENTS
         ...
         MOV    CX,ELEMENTS       ;SET UP LOOP COUNT
         ...
DATATEMP DW     ELEMENTS DUP(?)   ;TEMP FOR DATA
```

As you can see, we have used the constant elements not only to set up the count for a program loop, but also to reserve temporary storage for the data.

We can also use the EQU directive to form a synonym for another symbol, or a modification of that symbol's value. These are all valid EQUs.

```
MAX      EQU     0FFFH
SIZE     EQU     MAX
VALONE EQU     100
VALTWO EQU     VALONE*2
BUFSIZE EQU    25
BUFFER  DB      BUFSIZE DUP(?)
BUFEND EQU     BUFFER+BUFSIZE-1
```

The symbol BUFEND represents the last byte in the buffer. It has the same attributes as BUFFER with the exception of the offset value, which is modified to the offset of the last element. You should note that BUFEND was defined *after* BUFFER. If we had tried to define BUFEND before BUFFER, we would have created what is known as a *forward reference*. Some assemblers are sensitive to forward references, and their use will cause assembly errors. For example, forward references used with EQUs are not permitted with the Digital Research ASM-86 assembler. It is good programming practice to avoid forward references whenever possible.

SELF-CHECK

1) Define the following symbols:
   a) MAXDAT to 100
   b) COUNT to MAXDAT times 10
   c) CKCHAR to the ASCII character "Z"
2) Given the following EQUs:

```
FOO       EQU     10
DFOO      EQU     FOO*2
LFOO      EQU     DFOO+FOO
```

what are the actual numerical values assigned to the symbols FOO, DFOO, and LFOO?

3) Is the following a forward reference?

```
ALPHA     EQU     BETA
          MOV     AX, ALPHA
BETA      EQU     10
```

1) a) MAXDAT   EQU   100

   b) COUNT   EQU   MAXDAT*10

   c) CKCHAR   EQU   'Z'

2) FOO = 10, DFOO = 20, and LFOO = 30.
3) Yes, ALPHA cannot be defined until BETA is defined. The reference to ALPHA by the MOV instruction would not be a forward reference if ALPHA had been defined.

SEGMENT and ENDS Directives

You will recall that the 8086/8088 has four memory segments, CS for code, DS for data, SS for stack, and ES for extra use. Each of the four segments is capable of addressing 64K bytes of memory. These segments can be any size, up to the maximum of 64K, and they can also overlap. The management and assignment of data and instructions to these segments are the combined responsibilities of you as the programmer and of your computer's operating system. Your responsibility is to provide the assembler with information as to which parts of your program belong to which segment. The SEGMENT and ENDS directives are used to provide this information. They are always used as a pair.

Up to this point we have used the term segment to refer to the physical memory accessible through the appropriate segment register. From the perspective of the programmer, however, a segment can be any logical collection of assembly source statements. The total size must still be less than 64K bytes. Several logical segments can be combined into one physical segment so that they may be accessed by using only one segment base register. The total size of all these segments added together must also be less than 64K, or it would not be possible to reference them all. If we have logical segments whose individual sizes would add up to more than 64K, then we must make arrangements to provide different segment base registers for their reference. Or we must change the paragraph address of a single segment base register in such a manner that it will allow access to the appropriate area of memory.

The general form of the SEGMENT/ENDS directive is:

```
name   SEGMENT [align-type] [combine-type] ['class-name']
         .
         .
         .
name   ENDS
```

The name of the segment appears in the label field. This name is any proper user-defined symbol, and is used to refer to the segment itself. The ENDS directive marks the end of the segment. The name of the segment must be repeated with the ENDS directive.

The optional argument align-type specifies how the segment is aligned with byte, word, or paragraph boundaries. The default alignment is to a paragraph (multiple of 16 bytes). If you wish, this argument can be:

1. PARA—the default paragraph alignment.
2. BYTE—the segment can start at any address.
3. WORD—the segment must start on a word (even) address.

Some assemblers allow additional alignments, but these are of interest only to advanced programmers.

Combine-type is used to indicate how you would like logical segments to be combined to form a physical segment. The default is that the segment is not combinable. The exception is that separate parts of the same-named segment within a single assembly module will be combined. If we wish to combine several segments with the **same name** but in different assembly modules, we must specify a combine-type of PUBLIC. The linker is responsible for performing this operation. The combine-types are:

1. PUBLIC. Allows segments with the same name to be combined.
2. COMMON. Allows segments with the same name to be overlapped. This is identical to FORTRAN common usage.
3. STACK. Allows segments used as stacks to be overlapped. This is like COMMON except that the *ending* rather than starting addresses of the segments are aligned to the same memory address.

The optional class-name is a character string that can be used to inform the linker that segments with the same class-name should be located close to each other in physical memory.

Your particular assembler may allow other arguments with the SEGMENT directive. The Digital Research ASM-86 assembler uses a much simpler alternative to the SEGMENT/ENDS directives. Only a single code, data, stack, and extra segment can be specified. Four directives, CSEG, DSEG, SSEG, and ESEG, are used to mark the beginning of the respective segments. The segments are not named. Consult your assembler manual for details. The arguments I have mentioned are the most common and useful and should be adequate for most programming requirements.

You would normally specify your code segment as

```
CSEG    SEGMENT PUBLIC 'CODE'
          .
          .
          .
CSEG    ENDS
```

and your data segment as

```
DSEG    SEGMENT PUBLIC 'DATA'
          .
          .
          .
DSEG    ENDS
```

You must always provide a stack segment unless your operating system does it for you. A nice way to do this is to prime the stack segment with a pattern of data that can be easily recognized if you dump memory or use a debugger. The following stack should be adequate for most applications.

```
SSEG    SEGMENT STACK 'STACK'
        DB          64 DUP('STACK    ')
SSEG    ENDS
```

SELF-CHECK

1) How many bytes are reserved for the stack by the previous statements?
2) What is the purpose of the SEGMENT and ENDS directives?
3) What are the three alignment types discussed?
4) What combine-type is normally used for program code?

---

1) Since the character string is 8 bytes long, and the repeat count is 64, the total number of bytes reserved for the stack will be $8 \times 64 = 512$.
2) The SEGMENT and ENDS directives are needed to specify the logical segments to which program code or data belong. Ultimately these logical segments will become physical segments that will be referenced through a segment base register.
3) PARA—align on a paragraph boundary.
   BYTE—align on a byte boundary.
   WORD—align on a word boundary.
4) PUBLIC.

Although it is not usually necessary to split a logical segment into multiple parts within a single assembly module, it can be done.

```
MYSEG   SEGMENT PUBLIC
                     ;MYSEG PART ONE
              .
              .
MYSEG ENDS
;
XSEG    SEGMENT
              .
              .
XSEG    ENDS
;
MSEG    SEGMENT
              .        ;MYSEG PART TWO
              .
MSEG    ENDS
```

Both parts of MYSEG would be combined to form one logical segment. You do not have to specify any arguments for additional parts of the same-named segment. However, if they are specified, they must agree with the initial appearance of the segment.

The ASSUME Directive

In order for the 8086/8088 instructions to access the contents of a physical segment, the appropriate segment base register must be used. While it is always required that the code segment register be used to reference the instructions that are being executed, data elements can be accessed by *any* of the segment base registers, including the code segment base register. When you set up the various logical segments of your program, the assembler must know which segment base register you intend to use for each logical segment. It must have this information in order to ensure that either the default segment register used by the instruction is the proper register, or that a segment override prefix byte is needed. This special extra byte precedes an instruction.

The ASSUME directive is used to provide this information to the assembler. The general form of the ASSUME directive is:

```
ASSUME    segreg:segpart [,...]
ASSUME    NOTHING
```

Segreg is specified as one of the four segment base registers, CS, DS, SS, or ES. *Segpart* is the name of the logical segment that corresponds to the paragraph address contained in the segment base register. If NOTHING is specified for segpart, then we are indicating that that particular segment base register is not initialized to the paragraph address of any logical segment. ASSUME NOTHING, used alone, indicates that no segment base registers are initialized. This form can be used to clear previous assignments prior to new assignments.

If we have the following code and data segments:

```
MYCODE   SEGMENT PUBLIC 'CODE'
         .
         .
MYCODE   ENDS
;
MYDATA   SEGMENT PUBLIC 'DATA'
         .
         .
MYDATA   ENDS
```

we would use the following ASSUME directive:

```
ASSUME CS:MYCODE, DS:MYDATA
```

The actual initialization of the contents of the segment base registers is up to the programmer and the operating system. One fact should be made clear. If your program is executing, the code segment register must have been initialized properly. Otherwise, how would the instructions of your program be fetched by the CPU? This is always done by the operating system. In fact, your program cannot directly modify the contents of CS by an MOV instruction. The use of this register as the destination of an MOV is an illegal instruction.

The following instructions would initialize the data segment base register (DS) for the previous logical segment named MYDATA:

```
MOV    AX,MYDATA
MOV    DS,AX
```

We must use this pair of instructions because MYDATA is an immediate value, not a memory variable. You cannot move immediate data into a segment register with a single MOV instruction. These two instructions must be executed prior to referencing anything in the data segment. The appearance of the ASSUME directive must also precede the use of the data segment. You may, however, forward reference a logical segment name with the ASSUME directive. ASSUME directives can appear anywhere in your source program. They do not have to be inside a logical segment. As with many directives, ASSUME provides information only for the assembler and does not generate any machine code.

SELF-CHECK

1) Write an ASSUME directive to indicate that DS refers to segment MYDAT and ES refers to segment SPDAT.

2) Write the instructions necessary to set up the segment registers for access to the segments in Problem 1.

3) Is the following legal and reasonable?

```
        ASSUME  CS:FOO
FOO     SEGMENT PUBLIC
        MOV     AX, FOO
        MOV     CX,AX
          .
          .
          .
FOO     ENDS
```

1) ASSUME DS:MYDAT, ES:SPDAT

2) MOV   AX,MYDAT
   MOV   DS,AX
   MOV   AX,SPDAT
   MOV   ES,AX

3) No, CS cannot be the target of an MOV. It is not reasonable. CS must already be set up to refer to segment FOO, or these instructions would not be executing.

The END Directive

The END directive indicates to the assembler when there are no more source statements present for your program. The END directive is normally the very last line of your program. Additional lines may be present, but they will be ignored. While some systems have mechanisms to indicate the end of a file, the use of the END directive is a more positive mechanism since it does not depend on the specific system on which the assembler is running. It also allows program source to be moved from machine to machine, and assembler to assembler.

The format of the END directive is:

```
END     [expression]
```

The END directive serves another purpose. If the optional expression is present, it indicates the starting location of the program. This expression can be the name of a procedure or any address expression, so long as it is in the code segment. If your program consists of only one module, then the starting address must be specified. If your program consists of multiple modules, then only one module should have a starting address. If your program begins with the label BEGIN, then you would indicate this as follows:

```
BEGIN:      .
            <program>
            .
END     BEGIN     ;PROGRAM STARTS AT BEGIN
```

There are many more assembler directives included with most assemblers. Many of these concern the format of the assembly listing. For example, a TITLE directive allows you to include a title on the assembly listing. Since you really don't need these other directives to start programming, I have not attempted to cover them here. You should consult your assembler manual for details.

SELF-TEST

1) Do all assembler directives generate object bytes?
2) How can we tell an assembler directive from a machine instruction?
3) What are the attributes of a variable?
4) Can any character string be used with the DW directive?
5) Do all DB, DW, and DD directives have to be placed in a data segment?
6) Write the directives necessary to initialize memory to the following values:
   a) 100 words of 0's.
   b) An array of 100 words that is uninitialized.
   c) The string "aaaaaaaaaa"
7) What is the value of L for the following directives?

```
BUFF    DB      1, 2, 3, '123'
EBUFF   DB      0
L       EQU     EBUFF−BUFF
```

8) What is the maximum combined size of a group of segments?
9) Does it make sense to use the combine-type COMMON with program code segments?
10) What is the purpose of the ASSUME directive?

11) What do you think will happen if you do not set up the contents of the DS register prior to accessing a new data segment?

12) Can additional instructions be placed after the END directive?

1) No, many just provide information, such as the ASSUME directive.

2) Although assembler directives and instructions both appear in the operation field, the symbolic names of the assembler directives are distinct from the symbolic names used for machine instructions.

3) Segment, offset, and type.

4) No, only a 1- or 2-character string.

5) No, data-generating directives can be placed in any segment, including the code segment.

6) a) DW   100 DUP(0)

   b) DW   100 DUP(?)

   c) DB   'aaaaaaaaaa'
      or
      DB   10 DUP('a')

7) 6

8) 64K

9) No, because COMMON implies that the information in each segment is overlaid. Since a memory location can contain only one value, two different code segments cannot occupy the same locations in memory.

10) To establish the relationship between the segment base registers and specific logical segments.

11) Its previous value will be used, and all offsets will be to locations in the wrong part of memory.

12) No, the END directive indicates the last statement of the source program to be processed.

CHAPTER 7

The Stack

In this chapter we will examine the hardware stack implementation on the 8086/8088. A stack is a type of data structure. Computer scientists refer to data structures such as stacks as abstract data types. This is because we manipulate the data items contained on the stack by indirect means. In other words, we do not have to know the exact details of the particular abstract data structure in order to use it. The 8086/8088 provides a number of instructions that specifically manipulate data on the stack. Additionally, a number of other instructions use the stack to support their main functions. The CALL instruction that we have already used is a good example.

A stack is just about what its name implies, a stack of data elements. Below is an illustration of what an empty stack looks like.

As with a stack of dishes or books, we normally add or remove an item at the top of the stack. While it is possible to add or remove an element from the middle of a stack, this is not a proper use. The data elements that form a 8086/8088 stack are 16-bit quantities. Any data to be placed on the stack must be two bytes long. This must be kept in mind if we wish to place a single byte on the stack. The actual physical stack in memory is the stack segment. This is the physical segment whose paragraph address is contained in the stack segment base register. Additionally, the SP register is used to contain an offset into the stack segment, which is referred to as the *stack pointer*. This offset represents the top of the stack.

Each position in the stack is capable of holding a 16-bit value. The initial contents of the stack are of no significance. Whatever values are in the respective memory addresses are indicated by the question marks in the diagram. The actual length of the stack is up to the programmer, as long as the total length fits within a 64K physical segment.

Stack Instructions

While it might seem a bit confusing, the 8086/8088 stack is upside down. That is, when we add something to the stack, the elements are added to progressively lower memory addresses. For each 16-bit data element added to the stack, the value of the stack pointer (SP) is decremented by two. Remember, offsets or memory addresses are byte addresses, not word addresses. The instruction that adds something to the stack is the PUSH instruction. PUSH first decrements SP by two, then stores the source operand in the word pointed to by the stack pointer, SP. The instructions

```
MOV AX,1234H
PUSH AX
```

would result in the following stack:

	?	HIGH ADDRESS
SP⟶	1234H	
	?	
	?	
	?	
	?	
	?	
	?	
	?	
	?	LOW ADDRESS

We can PUSH a variable, a register, or a segment register. We can also push the flags with the PUSHF instruction. You cannot PUSH a constant directly onto the stack. To do this you must use the two instructions above.

In other words, you must go through a register. If we push another value onto the stack, let's say 5555H, the stack would look like this:

?	HIGH ADDRESS
1234H	
SP⟶ 5555H	
?	
?	
?	
?	
?	
?	
?	LOW ADDRESS

To retrieve elements from the stack, we use the POP instruction. Just as with the PUSH instruction, we can POP to a register, a variable, or a segment register. POP performs the inverse of a PUSH. The data element pointed to by the stack pointer is obtained from the stack and placed into the destination operand of the POP instruction. The stack pointer is then incremented by two. If we perform a POP BX on the above stack, the value 5555H is placed in the BX register. The stack then looks like this:

?	HIGH ADDRESS
SP⟶ 1234H	
5555H	BX ⟵ 5555H
?	
?	
?	
?	
?	
?	
?	LOW ADDRESS

Notice that the value 5555H has not been changed on the stack. However, it is below the stack pointer and is therefore no longer relevant. You might be tempted to try to access this value by modifying the stack pointer directly, for instance, with a SUB instruction. This is not a good idea. In fact, if hardware interrupts are enabled, the value might be changed without your being able to predict just when. We will cover hardware interrupts in Chapter 13. Always regard data below the stack pointer as lost forever.

What happens if we POP one too many elements from the stack? Since the 8086/8088 has no way of knowing how many valid elements are on the stack, it simply obtains the element pointed to by the stack pointer. If this points to an invalid stack element, then the value obtained is garbage. For this reason, all stack operations must be performed in pairs. A POP is matched with a previous PUSH. Due to the last-in first-out (LIFO) action of the stack, you must be careful to POP things in the reverse order they were PUSHed.

SELF-CHECK

1) Write the instructions necessary to push the value 100 onto the stack.
2) Write the instructions necessary to push the AX register onto the stack and pop it into the BX register.
3) Is this instruction legal?

    PUSH   AL

━━━━━━━━━━

1) MOV   AX,100
   PUSH   AX
2) PUSH   AX
   POP   BX
3) No, all values pushed onto the stack must be 16 bits.

Stack Applications

A stack can have many uses. In addition to its use for procedure calls, to be discussed in Chapter 8, the stack can be used by a programmer as a versatile temporary storage area. The only restriction is that the information stored on the stack must be saved and restored in reverse order.

Quite often one or more registers are needed for an operation, but these registers contain values that the programmer wishes to retain. These registers could be moved to other registers, if available, or saved in variable storage. The latter approach has the disadvantage that unless we define specific variable names for each such operation, we run the risk of accidentally using the same temporary storage location more than once. This would wipe out the previous value before it was restored. The problem does not exist with the stack because the stack can continue to grow, thus creating new temporary storage locations.

SELF-CHECK

Write the instructions necessary to save the AX, BX, CX, and DX registers, then restore them after performing some arbitrary operations.

```
PUSH    AX
PUSH    BX
PUSH    CX
PUSH    DX
...
...
...
POP     DX
POP     CX
POP     BX
POP     AX
```

(Note that the number of PUSH instructions matches the number of POP instructions and that the order of the registers is reversed when the POPs are performed.)

A stack can be used to reverse the order of a list of data items. The following program reverses a character string entered from the keyboard:

```
        MOV     AL,CR       ;PLACE A RETURN ON THE
                            ;STACK
        PUSH    AX          ;    "
NEXT:   CALL    GETC        ;GET A CHARACTER
        CMP     AL,CR       ;IS IT A RETURN?
        JE      REV         ;YES, NOW REVERSE
        PUSH    AX          ;NO, SAVE ON STACK
        JMP     NEXT        ;LOOP FOR MORE
REV:    CALL    NEWLINE     ;GO TO A NEW LINE
RNEXT:  POP     AX          ;GET A CHAR FROM THE
                            ;STACK
        CMP     AL,CR       ;FINISHED?
        JE      FINI        ;YES, EXIT
        CALL    PUTC        ;NO, OUTPUT THE CHAR
        JMP     RNEXT       ;LOOP FOR MORE
FINI:   CALL    NEWLINE     ;GO TO A NEW LINE
```

This program does not keep a count of the number of characters stored on the stack. Instead, the ASCII value of the carriage return is placed on the stack as a marker to indicate the start of the string. As we reverse the string, we will be moving from the end of the string to the start of the string. The carriage return tells us to stop POPping the stack. Any character code can be used, so long as it does not appear in the string itself.

SELF-CHECK

What would happen if we used a character code that appeared in the string?

When we tried to reverse the string, we would terminate the reverse loop prematurely. This would leave data on the stack that should have been removed. The consequences of this bad stack would affect the rest of your program. The very next POP performed would result in the wrong value. Since returns from procedures also use the stack, there would be disastrous results.

SELF-TEST

1) How many bytes must be pushed or popped from the stack at one time?
2) What register is used to hold the current offset into the stack segment?
3) How large can a stack segment be?
4) If we push something onto the stack, is the stack pointer incremented or decremented, and by what value?
5) Will this instruction work?

   PUSH   35

6) Write the instructions necessary to push the values 1 through 10 onto the stack.

1) Two.
2) The stack pointer, SP.
3) Up to 64K.
4) It is decremented by two.
5) No, a constant cannot be pushed onto the stack.

```
6)          MOV    AX, 1
    NEXT:   PUSH   AX
            INC    AX
            CMP    AX, 11
            JNE    NEXT
```

Procedures

When we write a program, we often find that we are repeating the same sequence of instructions in several different parts of the program. Unlike instructions that are repeated in a loop, these sequences of instructions must be repeated at different places in the program. Without the facility of *procedures*, we would be forced to repeat these sequences of instructions in our source code, and the machine instructions generated by the assembler would be repeated in memory as well. A larger program would result, and much extra typing would be needed.

Fortunately, we do have the ability to define procedures and to use the 8086/8088 instructions that support them. Any sequence of instructions can be defined as a procedure. Traditionally, a procedure has been called a *subroutine*. There is no difference, except that the terminology is more up to date if we use procedure rather than subroutine. The early high-level programming languages like FORTRAN used subroutine, while newer languages like PASCAL use procedure. However, you should not regard either a subroutine or a procedure in a high-level language as *exactly* the same thing in assembly language.

CALL and RET Instructions

As a simple example, let us say that we need to select the largest of three numbers. Assuming that these numbers are contained in the AX, BX, and CX registers, and that we want the largest value to be placed in the AX register, we might do it with the following instructions:

```
        CMP     AX,BX
        JGE     L1
        MOV     AX,BX
L1:     CMP     AX,CX
        JGE     L2
        MOV     AX,CX
L2:     .

        .
```

Each time we wished to perform this operation, we would have to repeat the above six instructions. We would also have to change the labels to make sure they were different for each repetition.

If we define these six instructions as a procedure, we can CALL the procedure each time we want to execute these six instructions. You have already used CALL for performing input/output, and you have been CALLing the appropriate input/output procedure all along. Here is how we would define the procedure with most assemblers:

```
BIGEST PROC
            CMP     AX,BX
            JGE     L1
            MOV     AX,BX
    L1:     CMP     AX,CX
            JGE     L2
            MOV     AX,CX
    L2:     RET
BIGEST ENDP
```

The general form of a procedure is:

```
procedure-name PROC  [type]
                  .
                  .
                  .
               RET
                  .
                  .
                  .
procedure-name ENDP
```

The assembler directives, PROC and ENDP, bracket the instructions that constitute the procedure. One or more RET instructions must appear in the procedure; otherwise, execution will fall out the bottom. The RET instruction can be the last instruction of the procedure, but it doesn't have to be. This will become clearer when we examine the exact mechanism by which procedures work.

Procedures can be defined at any convenient place in your program, but you should keep in mind that the instructions of the procedure appear in memory in exactly the position they appear in the source program. This means that you can't just stick a procedure into the middle of your main program. When the procedure's instructions are encountered, they will be executed in line. Normally, procedures are placed after your main program.

The procedure name is defined as a normal instruction label and corresponds to the address of the first instruction of the procedure. Your procedure BIGEST can be invoked from several places in your program by using a CALL instruction with the name of the procedure. For example:

```
            .
            .
            .
CALL    BIGEST
            .
            .
            .
```

CALL   BIGEST
.
.

Each time the CALL instruction is executed, the instructions of the procedure BIGEST are executed. How does the program find these instructions? The label BIGEST is used to tell the CALL instruction where to find the procedure. This can be thought of as equivalent to a simple JMP BIGEST instruction. So far, this is easy. But now consider what happens after the steps of BIGEST are executed. How do we get back to the instruction after the CALL? Which CALL? There may be quite a few. The answer lies with the use of the stack and the RET instruction.

Prior to transferring control to the procedure, the CALL instruction places the address of the instruction immediately following the CALL instruction itself on the stack. This is the instruction that should be executed when the instructions of the procedure are completed. Unless the procedure is in another code segment, only the offset of this return address is placed on the stack. When the RET instruction is executed in the procedure, the return address is POPped from the stack and placed into the Instruction Pointer (IP). This acts like another JMP instruction. The time control returns to the part of the program that CALLed the procedure, with execution continuing at the proper instruction. Figure 8 shows the sequence of events for a typical procedure call.

If the procedure is in another code segment, both the offset of the return address and the code segment register contents are placed on the stack. Also, when the procedure is CALLed, the code segment register is modified

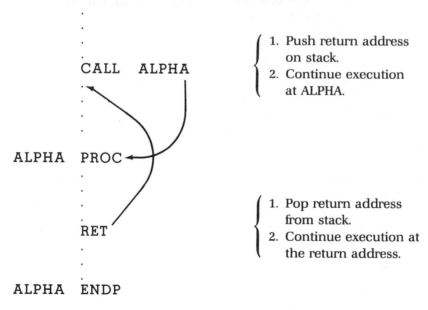

.
.
.
.
CALL   ALPHA
.
.
.
.

ALPHA   PROC
.
.
.
.
RET
.
.
.

ALPHA   ENDP

1. Push return address
   on stack.
2. Continue execution
   at ALPHA.

1. Pop return address
   from stack.
2. Continue execution at
   the return address.

Figure 8. Procedure calls.

by the CALL instruction to be set to the correct value. This value is that of the segment containing the procedure. Your assembler and linker handle the task of setting the appropriate segment register values, causing the proper CALL and RET instructions to be used. The optional argument to the PROC directive is used to indicate whether the procedure will be CALLed from another segment. In that case, the type of the procedure is FAR. The default is NEAR. Here is how we would set up a FAR procedure:

```
SEG1        SEGMENT PUBLIC 'CODE'
            .
            .
MYPROC  PROC FAR
            .
            .
            RET
MYPROC  END
SEG1        ENDS
;
SEG2        SEGMENT PUBLIC 'CODE'
            .
            .
            CALL  MYPROC  ;FAR CALL
            .
SEG2        ENDS
```

SELF-CHECK

1) Are subroutines and procedures essentially the same thing?
2) How does a procedure get control?
3) How does a procedure return control?
4) Where in your program can procedures be placed?
5) Write the instructions and directives for a procedure named CLEAR that clears the AX, BX, CX, and DX registers.

====

1) Yes, but they are not exactly the same as the subroutines and procedures of high-level languages.
2) By a CALL instruction.
3) By a RET instruction.
4) Anywhere, so long as they are not in the middle of code designed for sequential execution.
5)
```
CLEAR   PROC
        MOV     AX, 0
        MOV     BX, 0
        MOV     CX, 0
        MOV     DX, 0
        RET
CLEAR   ENDP
```

Passing Parameters

An assembly language procedure normally is free to access any variables within your program. In many cases you may want a procedure to use specific variables of your program as data for its operation. Some variables may be examined, but not modified by the procedure. Others may be modified. If a procedure specifically references variables other than those it uses for its own internal purposes, the programmer is stuck with always using these variables for passing data to and from the procedure. From your programming experience in a high-level language, you are probably wondering whether parameters or arguments can be passed to procedures in assembly language. The answer is yes. By allowing parameters, we can make a procedure more general through not always requiring the same specific variables to be used for passing data to or from the procedure.

Parameters or arguments can be passed to procedures in a great variety of ways. There are no standard methods, such as those used by high-level languages. The choice is up to the programmer. In fact, it is common practice for several different methods to be used in the same program. The simplest method is to place the parameters to be passed *to* the procedure in one or more of the registers. We did this with the BIGEST procedure. Under normal circumstances, one or more values are returned by the procedure. These values can be placed in the same or different registers, as we did with BIGEST. For procedures with a small number of parameters, the use of the registers is simple and efficient. Unfortunately, the number of registers is limited. Additionally, the use of registers may require copying data values to/from variables. We might also have to save values already in the registers before using them for parameters.

An alternative to the exclusive use of registers is to pass the address of a list of parameters to the procedure. This address is normally the offset of the list in the data segment. This offset can be passed in one of the registers, allowing a parameter list of arbitrary length, so long as all the parameters can be placed in memory at the same place. In Chapter 6, I briefly introduced the concept of using the BX register as a pointer. That means that BX contains the address of the operand rather than the operand itself. Only certain registers can be used in this manner. Specifically, we are limited to the use of BX, BP, SI, and DI. For now, let us always use BX. When advanced addressing modes are discussed in Chapter 9, the use of the other registers will be explained. Remember that to use BX in this way, we must enclose it in square brackets, [and]. Here is BIGEST rewritten to have parameters passed by the use of an argument list:

```
BIGEST PROC
        MOV   AX,[BX]      ;GET 1ST. ARG.
        ADD   BX,2         ;SET BX TO 2ND. ARG.
        CMP   AX,[BX]      ;COMPARE
        JGE   L1
        MOV   AX,[BX]
```

(continued on next page)

```
L1:       ADD   BX,2        ;SET BX TO 3RD. ARG.
          CMP   AX,[BX]
          JGE   L2
          MOV   AX,[BX]
L2:       RET
BIGEST  ENDP
```

We are still using the AX register to return the largest value. This actually has the advantage that none of the parameters passed to the procedure are modified. A fourth parameter, or return argument, could be used to return this value. Here is how we set up a CALL to BIGEST:

```
          .
          .
          MOV   BX, OFFSET ARG1
          CALL  BIGEST
          .                 ;AX NOW CONTAINS THE
          .                 ;LARGEST VALUE
          .
ARG1  DW    ?
ARG2  DW    ?
ARG3  DW    ?
```

The three arguments, ARG1, ARG2, and ARG3, would normally be set up in your data segment.

SELF-CHECK

Modify BIGEST to return the largest value in a fourth parameter.

====

```
BIGEST  PROC
          MOV   AX,[BX]      ;GET 1ST. ARG.
          ADD   BX,2         ;SET BX TO 2ND. ARG.
          CMP   AX,[BX]      ;COMPARE
          JGE   L1
          MOV   AX,[BX]
L1:       ADD   BX,2         ;SET BX TO 3RD. ARG.
          CMP   AX,[BX]
          JGE   L2
          MOV   AX,[BX]
L2:       ADD   BX,2         ;SET BX TO 4TH. ARG.
          MOV   [BX],AX
          RET
BIGEST  ENDP
```

The above technique works quite well if we can always group the parameters to a procedure in one list. If, however, some variables are used as parameters to several procedures and the argument lists are not the same, we are in trouble. Unless each procedure is written so that it knows which parameters to skip in the argument list, we can't use just one list. It would be poor programming practice to write procedures in this manner. A solution does exist. Instead of passing the actual parameters in the argument list, we can pass the addresses of the actual parameters. Just as we passed the address of the argument list in the BX register, we can pass the parameter addresses as word constants in the argument list. These values will correspond to the offset of each parameter in memory. It is a bit more work to get to the actual parameter. This is how BIGEST would be written:

```
BIGEST  PROC
        PUSH    BX
        MOV     BX,[BX]      ;GET 1ST. ARG. PTR.
        MOV     AX,[BX]
        POP     BX
        ADD     BX,2         ;SET BX TO 2ND. ARG. PTR.
        PUSH    BX
        MOV     BX,[BX]
        CMP     AX,[BX]      ;COMPARE
        JGE     L1
        MOV     AX,[BX]
L1:     POP     BX
        ADD     BX,2         ;SET BX TO 3RD. ARG. PTR.
        PUSH    BX
        MOV     BX,[BX]
        CMP     AX,[BX]
        JGE     L2
        MOV     AX,[BX]
L2:     POP     BX
        ADD     BX,2         ;SET BX TO 4TH. ARG. PTR.
        MOV     BX,[BX]
        MOV     [BX],AX
        RET
BIGEST  ENDP
   ;

            .
            .
        MOV     BX, OFFSET ARGLST
        CALL    BIGEST
            .
            .
   ;
ARGLST  DW      ARG1
        DW      ARG2
        DW      ARG3
        DW      ARG4
            .
ARG1    DW      ?
            .
ARG2    DW      ?
            .
ARG3    DW      ?
```

(continued on next page)

```
ARG4    DW    ?
```

Note that the stack is used to save the BX register temporarily while it is being used to hold the offset of each parameter. A PUSH and POP instruction do the job nicely. The MOV BX,[BX] instruction obtains each offset pointer in turn. You should also note that the parameters ARG1 through ARG4 do not have to be adjacent. They do not have to be in any order, but can be anywhere in the data segment. I want to remind you that for every PUSH instruction that is executed, a corresponding POP instruction is required. Otherwise, the stack will contain extra data items, and when the RET instruction is executed, the proper return address will not be obtained.

Saving and Restoring the Registers

Most procedures will require the use of one or more registers. If these registers are used to pass parameters, then the programmer is well aware of the use of these registers by the procedure. However, a register may be used by the procedure that is not used for a parameter. The programmer using the procedure must be aware of which registers are used if the contents are not preserved by the procedure. If the programmer is not careful, a bug is introduced. You must be sure that either the caller or the procedure saves and restores the appropriate registers.

The saving and restoring of the registers can be done by the caller or by the called procedure. Both have advantages and disadvantages. If saving and restoring the registers, the caller may be doing extra work. Let's say the caller is using most of the registers. The procedure being called may use only one or two. Unless the caller knows which registers are used by the procedure, all those being used must be saved and restored. The danger of assuming only certain registers are used by the procedure is that if the procedure is modified in the future to use an additional register, all calls must be checked to make sure a bug has not been introduced. This is a common source of bugs in assembly language programming. On the other hand, if the called procedure is responsible for saving and restoring the registers it uses, then the caller will never be doing extra work and the probability of errors will be sharply reduced. However, if the procedure uses a large number of registers, it may save and restore some of them that are not being used by a particular caller.

The technique of saving and restoring the registers is normally handled by using the stack. If the caller is saving and restoring the registers, the desired registers must be PUSHed prior to the CALL, then POPped after control returns from the procedure. Remember, the registers must be POPped in the reverse order from the PUSHes. If BX, CX, and DX are to be saved and restored by the caller, we would do it as follows:

```
PUSH   BX
PUSH   CX
PUSH   DX
CALL   MYPROC
POP    DX
POP    CX
POP    AX
```

SELF-CHECK

1) What are the disadvantages of using registers to pass parameters to a procedure?
2) Write a procedure called SUM that adds AH and AL and returns the result in AL.
3) Write a procedure and its call that add word variables A and B. Assume that A and B can be located next to each other in memory. Return the sum in AX.
4) Repeat the above problem, now assuming that A and B cannot be located next to each other in memory.

1) There are a limited number of them, and data may have to be copied to and from the registers.

```
2) SUM    PROC
          ADD    AL, AH
          RET
   SUM    ENDP

3) SUM    PROC
          MOV    AX, [BX]
          ADD    BX, 2
          ADD    AX, [BX]
   SUM    ENDP

          MOV    BX, OFFSET A
          CALL   SUM
          .
          .
   A      DW     ?
   B      DW     ?

4) SUM    PROC
          PUSH   BX
          MOV    BX, [BX]
          MOV    AX, [BX]
          POP    BX
          ADD    BX, 2
          MOV    BX, [BX]
          ADD    AX, [BX]
          RET
   SUM    ENDP
```

(continued on next page)

```
            MOV    BX, OFFSET ARGS
            CALL   SUM
            .
            .
            .
ARGS    DW     OFFSET A
        DW     OFFSET B
        .
A       DW     ?
        .
        .
B       DW     ?
```

Passing Parameters on the Stack

A technique of passing parameters to a procedure, often overlooked by assembly language programmers, is that of using the stack. If parameters are PUSHed onto the stack by the CALLer, the procedure can access them. The question is, how does this work if we consider that the return address is also PUSHed onto the stack by the CALL instruction? If the procedure were to POP values from the stack, the first value would be the return address. Unless this value is saved and later PUSHed back onto the stack, the procedure would not have the ability to return to its caller. While this could be done, a better method is possible.

Let us say that the caller wants to pass three parameters to a procedure and gives the following instructions:

```
PUSH   PARM3
PUSH   PARM2
PUSH   PARM1
CALL   MYPROC
```

The execution of these instructions would result in the following stack:

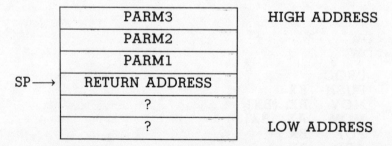

If we could access the stack without changing the stack pointer, SP, we could obtain the parameters. You can't use PUSH or POP since they automatically modify the stack pointer. The BP register is designed for just such a purpose. If we use BP as the source operand of an instruction, the stack segment is automatically referenced. To do this we can copy the value of SP into BP, using an MOV instruction. We can then increment or decrement BP as needed to reach the parameters. The following instructions demonstrate how we can obtain the three parameters of the preceding example:

```
MOV   BP,SP   ;GET A COPY OF SP
ADD   BP,2    ;SET TO POINT TO PARM1
MOV   AX,[BP] ;GET PARM1
 .

 .
ADD   BP,2    ;SET TO POINT TO PARM2
MOV   AX,[BP] ;GET PARM2
 .

 .
ADD   BP,2    ;SET TO POINT TO PARM3
MOV   AX,[BP] ;GET PARM3
 .

 .
RET
```

We had to add two to the initial value of BP to reach the correct offset of the address of the first parameter. Each time we add two to BP, we access the next parameter. Note that we had to PUSH the parameters on the stack in reverse order. Since we haven't modified SP, we can return to the caller with a simple RET instruction.

One problem remains. The parameters are still on the stack. The caller can POP the parameters:

```
POP   AX  ;PARM1
POP   AX  ;PARM2
POP   AX  ;PARM3
```

The caller can also modify SP directly:

```
ADD   SP,6
```

A third method is possible with the 8086/8088. An operand can be included with the RET instruction. If this operand is present, the RET instruction will automatically add this value to the stack pointer (SP) *after* the return address is obtained. The preceding example would be modified to use the following RET instruction:

```
RET   6    ;RETURN AND ADD 6 TO SP
```

SELF-CHECK

1) Modify BIGEST to use parameters passed on the stack, and return the result in the AX register.
2) Write the instructions necessary to call BIGEST.

```
1) BIGEST  PROC
           MOV    BP,SP        ;GET COPY OF SP
           ADD    BP,2         ;SET BP TO 1ST. ARG.
           MOV    AX,[BP]      ;GET 1ST. ARG.
           ADD    BP,2         ;SET BP TO 2ND. ARG.
           CMP    AX,[BP]
           JGE    L1
           MOV    AX,[BP]
   L1:     ADD    BP,2         ;SET BP TO 3RD. ARG.
           CMP    AX,[BP]
           JGE    L2
           MOV    AX,[BP]
   L2:     RET    6            ;CLEAN UP STACK AND
                               ;RETURN
   BIGEST  ENDP
2) PUSH    VAL1
   PUSH    VAL2
   PUSH    VAL3
   CALL    BIGEST
   . . .                ;AX HAS THE LARGEST VALUE
```

It doesn't matter in what order you PUSH the three values since BIGEST returns the result in the AX register, not a parameter.

SELF-TEST

1) When a CALL is executed, what actions take place?
2) What actions take place when a RET is executed?
3) Explain the difference between calls and returns to near and far procedures.
4) What is wrong with the following?

```
CRAZY   PROC
        PUSH    AX
        ADD     AX, BX
        RET
CRAZY   ENDP
```

5) The following procedure is designed to double the AX register and return the result in BX. What is a possible danger with the following procedure if the caller assumes that no registers are changed?

```
DOUBLE  PROC
        ADD     AX, AX
        MOV     BX, AX
        RET
DOUBLE  ENDP
```

6) Write a procedure named SKIPLINES that outputs blank lines specified by a count contained in the AX register.
7) If we pass parameters on the stack, what two methods can be used to clean up the stack?

8) The following instructions are not equivalent to RET 10. Explain why.

```
ADD   SP, 10
RET
```

9) What instructions *would* perform the equivalent of RET 10?

10) Write a procedure named PAIRS that outputs two values on a line. VAL1 is output first, then VAL2, followed by a new line. These values are passed on the stack by the following instructions:

```
PUSH   VAL1
PUSH   VAL2
CALL   PAIRS
```

It might help to draw the stack.

1) The return address is pushed onto the stack, and control transfers to the location specified by the operand of the call.

2) The return address is popped from the stack, and control transfers to the return address.

3) With a far procedure, both the segment and offset of the return address are pushed onto the stack, and control transfers to the segment and offset of the procedure. The return uses the segment and offset on the stack to locate the return address. Since a near procedure is within the current code segment, only the offset of the return address is pushed onto the stack.

4) There is no matching POP to the PUSH instruction; therefore the RET instruction will not obtain the correct return address.

5) The AX register is not saved and restored by the procedure.

6)
```
SKIPLINES       PROC
           PUSH AX
NEXT:      CALL NEWLINE
           DEC  AX
           JNE  NEXT
           POP  AX
           RET
SKIPLINES       ENDP
```

7) The caller can use an ADD instruction to register SP, or the procedure can use the optional argument to the RET instruction.

8) The add must be performed *after* the return address is popped.

9)
```
POP    RADDR  ;GET RETURN ADDRESS
ADD    SP, 10 ;CLEAN UP STACK
PUSH   RADDR  ;PUT RETURN ADDRESS BACK
RET
```

The above instructions assume a near call and also that variable RADDR is private to the procedure.

```
10) PAIRS    PROC
             MOV    BP, SP
             ADD    BP, 4
             MOV    AX, [BP]
             CALL   OUTDEC
             MOV    AL, ' '
             CALL   PUTC
             SUB    BP, 2
             MOV    AX, [BP]
             CALL   OUTDEC
             CALL   NEWLINE
             RET
   PAIRS     ENDP
```

CHAPTER 9

Addressing Modes

Up to this point we have not discussed addressing modes in detail, but we have actually used a number of them. You will learn several more addressing modes in this chapter. The addressing mode refers to the particular form of the operand or operands of an instruction. For example, we have used a register, a constant, or a memory variable as an operand. These are actually different addressing modes. In fact, these three basic types of operands are the three general types of addressing possible with the 8086/8088 CPU.

All operands used by an instruction must be located either in memory or in a register. Even constants must be placed in memory as part of the machine instructions themselves. The actual location of the operand value is referred to as the *effective address* of the operand.

Register Addressing

If a register is designated as the source or destination of an instruction, then the operand value is the value contained in the register. In other words, the effective address of the operand is the register itself. Not every instruction allows the use of *all* of the registers. Generally, the segment registers CS, DS, SS, and ES are not allowed. MOV is one exception. With MOV a segment register can be either the source or destination operand, but not both. We can only PUSH or POP to a 16-bit register, such as AX or BX.

Some instructions have implicit register operands. The LOOP instruction decrements the CX register. No other register can be used by this instruction for counting purposes. When we discuss the shifts and rotates in Chapter 10, you will learn that if a register is used with these instructions, it must be the CL register.

Immediate Addressing

The formal name for the addressing mode used when a constant is an operand is *immediate addressing*. The operand value is immediately available with the instruction itself. The effective address of the operand is the location in memory of the one or more bytes that specify the constant value. These bytes are always a part of the instruction itself. The assembler is responsible for generating the appropriate bytes for each instruction. Immediate operands become part of the machine instructions generated. While it may be technically possible to have the program itself change the value of these bytes, it is not an acceptable practice. If the program code is placed in read-only memory (ROM), it is not possible to modify these bytes.

You must keep in mind that the value of an immediate operand must be available at assembly time. If symbolic names are used, they must all ultimately be derived from numeric constants. If one symbol is defined using another symbol, that symbol must have a constant value. For example,

```
ALPHA   EQU   25
BETA    EQU   ALPHA*3
```

defines BETA as a constant with a value of 75.

Expressions of arbitrary complexity are permitted as immediate operands, as long as the value of the expression has the precision expected for the instruction. If an 8-bit value is required, 16-bit values can be combined in an expression, as long as the final result can be expressed in 8 bits or less. If we define the following symbolic constants:

```
C1   EQU   10000
C2   EQU   10050
```

then the following instruction is legal:

```
MOV   AL,C2-C1
```

because C2—C1 has a constant value of 50, which will fit into an 8-bit register.

SELF-CHECK

Given the following constants:

```
C1   EQU   1000
C2   EQU   1
C3   EQU   20000
C4   EQU   25000
```

which of the following instructions are proper?
1) ADD   AL,C1-C2

2) MOV   AX,C3+C4

3) SUB   BX,C4-C3

4) SUB   AH,C4-C3-C1

5) ADD   AL,C2

---

1) Not proper since C1—C2=999, which cannot be contained in the 8-bit register AL.

2) Not proper. C3+C4=45000, which cannot be contained in the 16-bit register AX.

3) Proper. C4−C3=5000, which will fit into a 16-bit register.

4) Not proper.

5) Proper. The constant, one, will certainly fit into the 8-bit register AL.

Advanced Expressions

While you normally will not need operand expressions more complicated than simple addition, multiplication, or division, almost all 8086/8088 assemblers include the ability to construct much more complex expressions.

The following are the standard arithmetic operators:

+   addition
−   subtraction
*   multiplication
/   integer division
MOD   modulo

These are all binary operators with the exception of + and −, which may also act as unary operators. A binary operator requires both a left and a right operand:

operand OP operand

while a unary operator requires only a single operand:

OP operand

Division always results in an integer result, so any remainder is lost. The result is not rounded but truncated. The expression 3/2 therefore evaluates to 1. The modulo operator is specified as the character string MOD. No special single character is used. The MOD operator works like division, but the remainder is used as the result, rather than the integer portion of the division. Therefore, 7 MOD 2 evaluates to 1. 37 MOD 32 evaluates to 5.

Multiplication, division, and modulo are always performed before any addition or subtraction. This means they have a higher precedence. You must use parentheses to override the standard precedence rules. For example, 3+5*6 evaluates to 33, while (3+5)*6 evaluates to 48. If two operators have the same precedence, evaluation is performed from left to right.

Symbols can be used along with numeric constants in expressions. As I have already mentioned, symbols used in expressions must be defined as constants. A variable name can be used in an expression, but not all expressions using variable names are legal, even though they might appear so. I will get to this in the next section when we look at memory addressing. The following are all legal expressions:

```
ALPHA+5
(BETA*3)+(GAMMA MOD 256)
COUNT/3 MOD 5
```

Logical operators are also available with most assemblers. The standard logical operators are:

AND   logical "and"
OR   logical "or"
XOR   logical "exclusive or"
NOT   logical negation

The logical operators are normally used to perform bitwise operations. This means that the individual bits of the word or byte are treated independently from the word or byte as a whole. For example, if we want to obtain only the low-order four bits of an expression, we can use the AND operator:

expression AND 1111B

Closely related to the logical operators are the shift operators:

SHR   shift right
SHL   shift left

These two operators have the form:

expression SHR count
expression SHL count

where count specifies the number of bits to be shifted left or right. Zeros are always shifted in, and bits shifted off the end are lost.

Logical and shift operations will be covered in depth in Chapter 10 when the logical, shift, and rotate instructions are covered. The difference will be that the logical and shift operations used in assembler expressions are performed by the assembler at the time the program is assembled rather than when the program executes.

SELF-CHECK

Given the following:

```
ALPHA     EQU  100
BETA      EQU  25
GAMMA     EQU  2
```

what are the values of these expressions?

1) ALPHA*100+BETA

2) ALPHA MOD GAMMA+BETA

3) (ALPHA+2)*BETA−2

4) (BETA/3) MOD 5

5) (ALPHA+3)*(BETA MOD GAMMA)

6) ALPHA SHR GAMMA

7) BETA AND 7

8) GAMMA OR 3

1) 10,025
2) 25
3) 2,346
4) 3
5) 103
6) 25
7) 1
8) 3

Memory Addressing

If memory addressing is used for an operand, the effective address will be a location in memory. This location is specified by a segment and an offset within the segment. The following different types of memory addressing are possible:

1. Direct addressing.
2. Register indirect addressing.
3. Based addressing.
4. Indexed addressing.
5. Based index addressing.

We will now discuss each type of memory addressing in depth. As you will see, each type is especially suited to access particular data structures. The data structures will be introduced as examples for each addressing mode shown.

Direct Addressing
A direct address is specified by using a variable or label.

```
MOV   BX,VALUE
JMP   NEXT
```

are instructions that have simple direct addresses. In the case of the MOV instruction, VALUE is a variable whose effective address is located in the data segment. NEXT is a label located in the code segment. Expressions involving a label or variable are permitted.

```
MOV   BL,VALUE+3
```

places the third byte following VALUE in register BL. We must make sure that an expression involving a variable involves only adding or subtracting a constant value from the offset of the variable. The instruction

```
MOV   AX,VALUE*5
```

does not have meaning because the effective address depends on the specific offset of VALUE. If the position of VALUE is changed, as would be the case by adding or deleting a variable preceding VALUE, the instruction would have a different effective address. Most assemblers do not permit such address expressions. Remember, VALUE represents a location in memory, not a numeric constant.

Register Indirect Addressing

We used register indirect addressing in Chapter 8 to pass a pointer to a procedure. Remember that a pointer is the offset of a data item in memory. Normally this data item is found in the data segment. When we place an offset in a register and then use that register with indirect addressing, we access the item pointed to by the register. In other words, the value in the register represents the effective address of the operand. To specify to the assembler that register indirect addressing is desired, we merely enclose the register name in square brackets. Only certain registers can be used in this manner. BX, BP, SI, and DI are the only registers that can be used with register indirect addressing.

To use register indirect addressing, we place the offset of the memory location we want to reference into the appropriate register. In order to obtain the offset of a variable, a special operator, OFFSET, is provided. The expression OFFSET ALPHA has a value equivalent to the offset of the variable ALPHA. Once we have set up the offset in the register, we can add or subtract a relative offset from the register's contents in order to reposition ourselves to a different memory location. The instructions ADD or SUB can be used for large movements, and INC or DEC can be used for repositioning by plus or minus a single byte.

One natural application of register indirect addressing is in the access of an array. A simple array is a data structure in which all elements are of the same data type, for example, all are words. If we set up a register to point to the first element of the array, we can access each element by incrementing the register. For example:

```
        MOV   BX, OFFSET ARRAY    ;INITIALIZE POINTER
        MOV   AX, [BX]            ;GET ARRAY ELEMENT
        .                         ;USE THE ELEMENT
        ADD   BX,2               ;POSITION TO NEXT
                                  ;ELEMENT
        .
        MOV   AX, [BX]            ;GET NEXT ARRAY
                                  ;ELEMENT
        .                         ;ETC.
        .
ARRAY   DW    1, 2, 3, 4, 5       ;A FIVE ELEMENT
                                  ;ARRAY
                                  ;   OF WORDS
```

In this case we had to add two to the pointer in BX because the array was an array of words.

SELF-CHECK

Write a program to output the contents of a numerical array of words until a zero value is found.

```
          MOV   BX, OFFSET ARRAY
NEXT:     MOV   AX, [BX]
          CMP   AX, 0
          JE    DONE
          CALL  OUTDEC
          CALL  NEWLINE
          ADD   BX, 2
          JMP   NEXT
DONE:     .

ARRAY DW  23,36,2,100,32000,54,0
```

Quite often a program requires the moving of data from one array to another. There are many ways to accomplish this task. When we discuss the string instructions in Chapter 11, you will find that the 8086/8088 has a powerful array-moving capability. For now, let us assume that we will use register indirect addressing. If we initialize two registers, each with a pointer to the start of an appropriate array, we can advance through the array by simultaneously incrementing the two registers. Let's assume that we wish to move COUNT bytes from ARRAY1 to ARRAY2. In this case, we have specified a 100-byte array. We can use the SI and DI registers. Here is the program:

```
COUNT    EQU   100
         MOV   SI, OFFSET ARRAY1
         MOV   DI, OFFSET ARRAY2
         MOV   CX, COUNT
NEXT:    MOV   AL, [SI]
         MOV   [DI], AX
         INC   SI
         INC   DI
         LOOP  NEXT
         .

ARRAY1   DB    COUNT DUP(?)
ARRAY2   DB    COUNT DUP(?)
```

Register indirect addressing can be used for either the source or destination operand of an instruction, but not both. It would be nice if we could write the following instruction

```
MOV   [DI],[SI]
```

but we can't. Your assembler would indicate an error.

Segment Overrides

If we use BX, SI, or DI with register indirect addressing, the effective address is a location in the data segment. The BP register is an exception. If BP is used with register indirect addressing, the data item is not assumed to be in the data segment, but instead is found in the stack segment. Sometimes this is not what the programmer desires. For example, you may wish to use a value contained in the extra segment. Normally the assembler would know that you were referencing a particular segment by the use of a particular variable name because the segment associated with the variable is one of the variable's attributes. This is not the case when a register contains a pointer. The segment information is not present.

The 8086/8088 CPU is equipped with a special facility to override the default segment associated with a particular addressing mode. A *segment override* prefix can be specified in your assembler source statement. This segment override prefix generates a special prefix byte that precedes the instruction's operation code in memory, forcing the CPU to use the segment you specify. The four segment overrides are: CS:, DS:, SS:, and ES:. These overrides correspond to the segment register designations. Normally

```
MOV   AX,[BX]
```

would refer to an item in the data segment. However,

```
MOV   AX,ES:[BX]
```

forces the offset contained in BX to be used as an offset into the current extra segment. A segment override prefix can be used with any of the memory addressing modes we have discussed or will discuss.

Based Addressing

Based addressing is similar to register indirect addressing, except that a displacement can be added to the register value, forming the offset to be used as the memory address. There are a number of ways to specify this displacement, but not all these methods work with all assemblers. The following are the most common:

```
MOV   AX, [reg + disp]
MOV   AX, [reg] [disp]
MOV   AX, disp [reg]
MOV   AX, [reg] + disp
```

where *reg* and *disp* refer to the appropriate register and displacement. The displacement must be a constant. It cannot be a variable. If it were, we would be attempting to access a variable whose offset was the sum of the offsets of two other variables. This would not make sense. (On the Digital Research ASM-86 assembler, only the last two methods can be used.)

In Chapter 8 we obtained the parameters to a procedure by passing a pointer to the base of an argument list in register BX. We then added an appropriate displacement to obtain each argument in turn. If we wish to reference the same parameter at several points in the program, we must continually modify the value in BX to refer to the proper offset in memory. Based addressing allows us to do this without actually changing the register's value. If we assume that BX points to a parameter list of words, we can access various parameters as follows:

```
MOV  AX, [BX]        ;ARG 1
.
MOV  AX, [BX+2]      ;ARG2
.
MOV  AX, [BX+10]   ;ARG 6
```

It doesn't matter if the arguments are a mixture of byte and word data if we make sure that the displacement is computed correctly. Based addressing can be used to access any element of an array on a random basis. All we have to do is to place the base address (offset) of the array in a register and use based addressing.

SELF-CHECK

Write the instructions necessary to access the seventh character in the character string "based addressing" and place it in register DL.

```
MOV  BX, OFFSET CSTRING
MOV  DL, [BX+6]              ;GET SEVENTH CHAR.
.

CSTRING DB    'BASED ADDRESSING'
```

Often we may want to construct an array consisting of more complex data elements than bytes or words. These elements may, in fact, be arrays themselves. Let's assume, for instance, that we wish to construct a simple table of the names and ages of certain individuals. Each element of this table would consist of the person's name, a character string, and his/her age, a byte. We can assume no one can live to be over 255 years, so a byte conserves space over the use of a word variable. Each element can be defined as:

```
DB  32 DUP(?)   ;NAME
DB  ?           ;AGE
```

This assumes that names can be specified in 32 characters or less. Each element of our name list will be 33 bytes long. If we want to enter specific names and ages, we might set up the following table:

```
NAMES   DB    'TOM'
        DB    40
        DB    'KRISTIN'
        DB    3
        DB    'ERIN'
        DB    2
```

(continued on next page)

etc.
```
LENGTH    EQU    (OFFSET $ − OFFSET NAMES) / 33
```

The constant, LENGTH, is equal to the number of entries in the array. We could have specified the number directly, but this would not be the best way. If we add or delete an entry from the table, we might forget to fix the value of LENGTH. The way I have specified LENGTH, it is automatically recomputed. The symbol $ represents the current value of the location counter. It is the offset of the next memory location to be used. In other words, it is the first location after the last data element in our table. Subtracting the offset of the first element of the table would give us the size in bytes. By dividing by 33, we have computed the number of entries in the table.

If register BX is set to point to a specific array, a displacement of zero gives us the name; a displacement of 32 gives us the age. In order to advance from one table entry to the next, we must add 33 to the pointer in BX. The following program will print out the ages in our table.

```
        MOV    CX, LENGTH          ;SET UP COUNTER
        MOV    BX, OFFSET NAMES    ;GET BASE OF TABLE
NEXT:   MOV    AH, 0               ;ZERO HIGH BYTE
        MOV    AL, [BX+32]         ;GET AGE
        CALL   OUTDEC              ;OUTPUT
        CALL   NEWLINE
        ADD    BX, 33              ;ADVANCE TO NEXT
                                   ;ENTRY

        LOOP   NEXT
```

In this example I have used the actual numerical displacement values of the table entries in the program. If we want to modify the table by adding an additional data item such as the person's sex, some of these numerical constants will change. The length of a table entry will not remain at 33. Since we may be referring to the table from several different points in the program, we would have to modify the program at a number of places. We might forget one or make a mistake while editing the program. To ensure consistency and to reduce the editing time for changes, the EQU directive can be used to allow symbolic constants to be used. If we add the appropriate EQUs to the program, it can be written as follows:

```
NAME     EQU    0
AGE      EQU    32
ENTLEN   EQU    33
;
         MOV    CX, LENGTH          ;SET UP COUNTER
         MOV    BX, OFFSET NAMES ;GET BASE OF TABLE
NEXT:    MOV    AH, 0               ;ZERO HIGH BYTE
         MOV    AL, [BX+AGE]        ;GET AGE
         CALL   OUTDEC              ;OUTPUT
         CALL   NEWLINE
         ADD    BX, ENTLEN          ;ADVANCE TO NEXT
                                    ;ENTRY

         LOOP   NEXT
```

SELF-CHECK

1) What registers may be used with register indirect addressing?
2) Write an instruction that will move a byte of data to register AL from an offset in the extra segment pointed to by register BX.
3) Write an instruction that will initialize register BX to the offset of variable MYDAT.
4) The following is the layout of a data record:

```
PARTNO  DW   ?
PNAME   DB   16 DUP(?)
COUNT   DW   ?
```

Write the instruction necessary to access COUNT, assuming that BX is set up to point to the start of the record in memory.

5) What will be the contents of register AX after executing the following instructions?

```
        MOV   BX, OFFSET TABLE
        ADD   BX, ENTRY
        MOV   AX, [BX]
        .
        .
        .
TABLE   DW    10, 20, 30, 40, 50
ENTRY   DW    3
```

1) BX, BP, SI, and DI

2) MOV AL, ES:[BX]

3) MOV BX, OFFSET MYDAT

4) MOV AX, [BX+18]

5) 40

Indexed Addressing

With based addressing we placed the address (offset) of the data structure into the register and used the displacement as an index into the data structure. Indexed addressing works in a similar manner, except the displacement is placed in the register, and the base address of the data structure is specified. The SI and DI registers are normally used for indexed addressing, although BX and BP can also be used. The general form for index addressing is

```
    variable [reg]
```

or

```
    variable [reg + displacement]
```

An optional displacement (constant) can also be added to the index value. For those readers who have used arrays in high-level languages, this format should look quite familiar. If the variable name represents a simple array, the register contains the index of the desired element. If we define an array, VALS

```
VALS   DB   100 DUP (?)
```

we can access any array entry by loading an index register with the desired entry and using indexed addressing.

```
MOV   SI,32
MOV   AL, VALS [SI]
```

would place the 33rd array element in the AL register. The 33rd element is obtained because the first array element is at index value zero. If you desire an array based on one rather than zero, a displacement of one can be subtracted:

```
MOV   SI,32
MOV   AL, VALS [SI−1]
```

In this case, the 32nd array element is obtained.

You must remember that the index is always a byte index. Unless the array is an array of bytes, you will have to make sure that the index value is multiplied by the size of the array elements. Since we quite often step through arrays sequentially, this means adding the element size to the index register to advance to the next element.

It may seem to you that either based addressing or indexed addressing is equally easy to use for the same tasks. Sometimes this is true, but there are many times when we wish to access a number of different data structures with the same index. In order to do this with based addressing, we must reload the register before accessing each different data structure. We could use several different registers, but then they would not be availble for other uses. If we want to add two byte arrays, ARRAY1 and ARRAY2, element by element, leaving the result in ARRAY2, we could do it quite easily with the following:

```
        MOV   SI,0
        MOV   CX,COUNT        ;COUNT IS ARRAY SIZE
NEXT:   MOV   AL,ARRAY1 [SI]
        ADD   AL,ARRAY2 [SI]
        MOV   ARRAY2 [SI],AL
        LOOP  NEXT
```

SELF-CHECK

Rewrite the previous program using register indirect addressing, with only one register for addressing.

```
        MOV   CX,COUNT
        MOV   BX,OFFSET ARRAY1
        MOV   ARRAY1P,BX
```

```
                    MOV     BX,OFFSET ARRAY2
                    MOV     ARRAY2P,BX
NEXT:               MOV     BX,ARRAY1P
                    MOV     AL,[BX]
                    INC     BX
                    MOV     ARRAY1P,BX
                    MOV     BX,ARRAY2P
                    ADD     AL,[BX]
                    MOV     BYTE PTR [BX],AL
                    INC     BX
                    MOV     ARRAY2P,BX
                    LOOP    NEXT
;
;IN DATA SEGMENT
;
COUNT      EQU      array_size
ARRAY1     DB       COUNT DUP (?)
ARRAY2     DB       COUNT DUP (?)
ARRAY1P    DW       ?
ARRAY2P    DW       ?
```

Note: This program could have been simplified if I had allowed more than one register to be used for addressing, but then my point would not have been made. You will notice that two temporary storage locations are used to save the current pointer values, which are alternately moved to register BX. Other registers could be used as temporaries, but this would be just as bad as using these additional registers for addressing.

Based Indexed Addressing

The final addressing mode we will discuss is based indexed addressing. As the name implies, this addressing mode is a combination of both based addressing and indexed addressing. We use either BX or BP in combination with SI or DI. We cannot use BX and BP, nor can we use SI and DI. We can place the base of a data structure in register BX and use SI as the index into the data structure. For example:

```
                    MOV     CX, COUNT
                    MOV     BX, OFFSET ARRAY
                    MOV     SI, 0
        NEXT:       MOV     AL, [BX] [SI]
                      .
                      .
                      .
                    INC SI
                    LOOP    NEXT
```

will access COUNT bytes from an array named ARRAY. The advantage of this addressing mode is that we can access the elements of an array without using the array name. The address of the array might be passed as a parameter to a procedure.

If our data structure has multiple dimensions, we can use based indexed addressing. We place the offset of the portion of the structure we wish to access in BX, then use SI or DI to index this portion. For example, we may have a data structure consisting of information about a group of employees. The information for each employee consists of a certain number of bytes. Let's say each employee record takes 100 bytes. If the name of this data structure is EMPLDAT, we can obtain information about employee number 5 by using based indexed addressing. If the first employee is at offset 0, then we would use the following instructions:

```
       MOV    CX, 100
       MOV    BX, (5−1)*100
       MOV    SI, 0
NEXT:  MOV    AL, EMPLDAT [BX] [SI]
       .
       .   ;ACCESS EACH BYTE OF THE RECORD
       .
       INC    SI
       LOOP   NEXT
```

An optional displacement can also be used with based indexed addressing.

Sometimes we wish to obtain the effective address of an operand rather than the operand itself. The load effective address (LEA) instruction is designed for that purpose. It works like the MOV instruction, except the offset of the effective address is moved to the destination, rather than the contents of the effective address. The source operand must be a memory reference, and the destination must be a 16-bit register. Any addressing modes may be used for the source as long as they result in a memory reference. For example:

```
LEA   AX, ARRAY
```

is equivalent to

```
MOV   AX, OFFSET ARRAY
```

Here is an example where we cannot use a MOV:

```
LEA   AX, STRUCT [BX] [SI]
```

This is equivalent to the following instructions:

```
MOV   AX, OFFSET STRUCT
ADD   AX, BX
ADD   AX, SI
```

Two other instructions can be used to form pointers, the load pointer using ES, LES, and the load pointer using DS, LDS. Both of these instructions must have a source operand in memory and a destination operand that is one of the 16-bit general purpose registers. The memory operand must be a 32-bit double word. The first 16 bits of this double word must be a valid segment offset. The second 16 bits must be the paragraph address of a segment. The offset value is loaded into the general register, and the paragraph address is loaded into ES or DS, depending on which instruction is used. This is a simple way of obtaining a pointer to a data element in another segment. We can load a segment base register and a general purpose register in one operation.

We can use the DD directive to set up the 32-bit pointer. For example, the following instructions can be used to access the array XARRAY which is not in the current data segment.

```
SEG1       SEGMENT 'DATA'
           .
           .
XARRAY  DB         100 DUP (?)
SEG1       ENDS
;
SEG2       SEGMENT 'DATA'
           .
           .
XPTR      DD         XARRAY
           .
SEG2       ENDS
;
CSEG       SEGMENT 'CODE'
           .
           .
           ASSUME  DS:SEG2
           .
           LES        BX, XPTR
           MOV        AL, ES: [BX]
           .
CSEG       ENDS
```

As I mentioned in Chapter 4, the 8086/8088 uses the same mnemonics for byte and for word instructions. Usually it is clear from the operands of the instructions whether a byte or word instruction is needed. However, certain addressing modes may not provide this information. For example, the instruction

```
MOV   AL, [BX]
```

must be a byte instruction because register AL is specified. Register BX must point to a byte variable. But what about the following?

```
MOV   [BX], 0
```

Do we want to zero the byte or word pointed to by BX? There is no way for the assembler to tell. Only the programmer knows what was intended.

Fortunately, there is a mechanism with which we can tell the assembler that an effective address is a byte or a word. We have two special operators:

1. **BYTE PTR.** Specifies a byte operand.
2. **WORD PTR.** Specifies a word pointer.

The previous instruction could be written to specify either a byte or word destination with the following:

```
MOV   BYTE  PTR [BX], 0
MOV   WORD PTR [BX], 0
```

These operators can be used with more complicated addressing modes, such as based indexed addressing. For example,

```
ADD  WORD PTR [BX] [SI+5], 2
```

will add the constant 2 to a word in memory.

If your assembler can't determine the particular instruction to generate, it will give you an error on the line containing the instruction. You will have to edit the program and provide the correct information.

SELF-TEST

1) What are the three basic types of operands?
2) What is the effective address of the destination of the following instructions?
   a) MOV AX, 0
   b) MOV BYTE PTR [BX], 0
   c) MOV VAL, 0
3) What are the default segments referenced by register indirect addressing, using BX, BP, SI, or DI?
4) What are the allowable segment override prefixes?
5) You wish to move the sixth word of an array named BLOCK to register DX. Write the instructions necessary to do this with
   a) register indirect addressing.
   b) based addressing.
   c) indexed addressing.
6) Write a program necessary to reverse the elements of a 100-byte array named ELEMS.
7) Which of the following are legal?
   a) MOV AH, BX
   b) MOV AH, [BX]
   c) MOV [BX], [SI]
   d) MOV AX, [BX] [SI]
   e) MOV AX, [SI] [DI]
   f) MOV BYTE PTR [BX], 1000
   g) MOV EMPLDAT [BX] [SI], ES:AX

8) What won't the following work?

```
MOV   BX, OFFSET DATTBL [SI]
```

1) Registers, constants, and memory variables.
2) a) Register AX.
   b) A byte in memory at an offset in the data segment specified by the value of register BX.
   c) The location in memory of variable VAL.
3) BX, SI, and DI all reference the data segment. Register BP references the stack segment.
4) CS:, ES:, DS:, or SS:
5) a)
```
MOV   BX, OFFSET BLOCK
ADD   BX, 10
MOV   DX, [BX]
```

   b)
```
MOV   BX, OFFSET BLOCK
MOV   DX, [BX]+10
```

   c)
```
MOV   SI, 10
MOV   DX, BLOCK [SI]
```

6)
```
        MOV   CX, 50
        MOV   SI, 99
        MOV   DI, 0
NEXT:   MOV   AL, ELEMS [SI]
        MOV   AH, ELEMS [DI]
        MOV   ELEMS [DI], AL
        MOV   ELEMS [SI], AH
        DEC   SI
        INC   DI
        LOOP  NEXT
```

7) a) Not legal. Register sizes don't match.
   b) Legal.
   c) Not legal. Both source and destination cannot be memory references.
   d) Legal.
   e) Not legal. SI and DI cannot be used together.
   f) Not legal. The destination should be a word.
   g) Not legal. Improper use of the segment override prefix.
8) The OFFSET operator computes the offset value of the operand at assembly time. With indexed addressing the value is not known at assembly time. The LEA instruction should be used.

```
LEA   BX, DATTBL [SI]
```

Logical, Shift, and Rotate Instructions

In this chapter we will examine a group of instructions that can manipulate the individual bits of a byte or a word by performing logical operations, such as AND and OR. You will also learn how shift and rotate instructions can change the positions of all the bits in a byte or word in interesting ways.

Truth Tables

There are four logical operations that have corresponding 8086/8088 instructions: NOT, AND, OR, XOR (exclusive or). These four logical operations can be described by the use of a truth table. AND, OR, and XOR are operations that require two operands: NOT requires only one. When used as 8086/8088 instructions, these logical operations act on *all* the bits of the bytes or words in parallel. However, the action on individual bits or on bit pairs is the same. Because of this fact, we can describe each operation with a truth table consisting of, at most, a pair of bits.

The NOT logical operation essentially reverses ones and zeros. In other words, a one becomes a zero and a zero becomes a one. The truth table would look like this:

	Operand	
	0	1
Result	1	0

NOT

The AND operation takes two operands. The resulting bit is a one only if both the operand bits are one.

Operand 1

		0	1
Operand 2	0	0	0
	1	0	1

AND

OR results in a one if either of the operand bits is a one.

Operand 1

		0	1
Operand 2	0	0	1
	1	1	1

OR

XOR is just like OR, except that the result is a zero if *both* operands are one.

Operand 1

		0	1
Operand 2	0	0	1
	1	1	0

XOR

The general form of the logical instructions is exactly the same as for ADD or SUB. Both a source and a destination must be specified. These can be variables, constants, or registers. However, just as with ADD or SUB, both operands cannot be variables. The corresponding bits of the source and destination operands are used to form the result that is stored in the destination, which must be a register or variable.

For example, we can execute the following instructions:

```
MOV   AL, 55H
AND   AL, 64H
```

The following logical operation is thus performed:

```
        01010101
AND     01100100
        01000100
```

The result, 44H, would be left in the AL register. The operation has been shown in binary to make what is happening clearer. The bits in each column are operated on separately.

What is the result of the following logical operations?

1) 1234H AND 0FF00H

2) 7FFFH XOR 654FH

3) NOT 55AAH

4) AAAAH OR 5555H

5) Write a logical instruction that will clear register AX.

6) Write a logical instruction that will ensure that the high-order 3 bits of register DX are ones.

7) Write a logical instruction that will ensure that the low-order 4 bits of register BL are zeros.

8) Write a logical instruction that will set the bits of register AX in such a way that a bit is set to one if it differs from the corresponding bit in register BX.

---

1) 1200H

2) 1AB0H

3) AA55H

4) FFFFH

5) XOR AX, AX or AND AX, 0

6) OR DX, 0E000H

7) AND BL, 0F0H

8) XOR AX, BX

Shifts

The logical instructions can be used to manipulate individual bits or groups of bits within a word or byte. However, the positions of the bits that are manipulated remain the same. We sometimes want to treat all the bits of a byte or word as a group and change their positions. We can imagine a virtually unlimited number of possible operations. Since it would not be practical to implement a machine instruction for every possible reorganization of the bits of a word or byte, two of the most useful operations are implemented, namely, shifts and rotates.

The bits of a word or byte are normally numbered as follows:

Byte

7 6 5 4 3 2 1 0

Word

15	14	13	12	11	10	9	8	7	6	5	4	3	2	1	0

We can shift the bits of a word or a byte to either the left or the right. For each shift of one position, all the bits move left or right, each bit replacing the bit previously occupying that position. The shift looks like this:

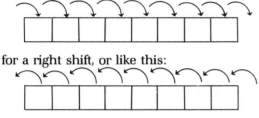

for a right shift, or like this:

for a left shift.

You are probably wondering what happens to the bit that falls off the end of a left or right shift. You are also probably wondering whether a one or zero bit is shifted into the high-order bit position of a right shift or the low-order position of a left shift. The answer to the first question is quite simple. If we shift left or right, the bit that falls off the end is saved in the carry flag (CF). This is either bit 7 for a byte shift or bit 15 for a word shift if we are shifting left, and bit 0 for all right shifts.

If we shift left, a bit with a zero value is *always* shifted into the lower-order bit position of the byte or word. This is the bit 0 position. When we shift right, two results are possible. If we use the logical shift right instruction (SHR), a zero bit is shifted into the high-order bit position. If we use the arithmetic shift right instruction (SAR), the value of the high-order bit is shifted into itself. In other words, the value of the high-order bit is not changed. This is what these shifts look like:

SHR

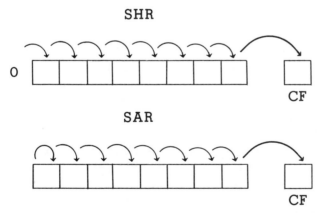

CF

SAR

CF

The purpose of the arithmetic shift is to preserve the sign bit. You will recall that the sign bit is the high-order bit when using two's complement representation. One use of the shift instructions is to multiply or divide a number by a power of two. Without the arithmetic forms of the shift instructions, incorrect values would result. The corresponding mnemonics for the left shifts are SHL and SAL. These are not two different instructions; they are two different mnemonics for the same machine instruction. The reason is that there is no difference between a logical shift or an arithmetic shift when we shift left.

There are two forms for the shift instructions:

```
opcode dest, 1
```

and

```
opcode dest, CL
```

where opcode is the appropriate shift instruction and dest is either a memory variable or a register. The first form specifies a shift of only one bit, while the second form allows a shift equal to the value contained in the CL register. You *must* use the CL register. No other register can be specified. You *cannot* use a constant value other than one with the first form. You could, if you wanted, load the CL register with a value of one and use the second form. This would have the same result as the first form but has the disadvantage that it requires the CL register and the additional instruction to load it. Also, the value in CL may have to be saved and restored. Because of this, it is sometimes better to repeat a shift instruction with the first form for low-number shifts rather than to load the CL register and use the second form.

If the AX register contains 5432H, the shift

```
SAL      AX,1
```

results in 0A864H in AX. Similarly,

```
SHR      AX,1
```

results in 2A19H. And

```
MOV      CL,8
SHL      AX,CL
```

will shift AX left by eight bits. This will shift in eight zeros, and the value in AX after the shift will be 3200H.

As I mentioned earlier, one use of the shift instructions is to multiply or divide by a power of two. Even though the 8086/8088 has a number of multiply and divide instructions, it is sometimes easier and faster to use a shift. This only works when multiplying or dividing by a power of two. A left shift will multiply by 2^n where n is the number of bits to shift. A right shift (be sure to use SAR) will divide by 2^n. Since the bits shifted off the end are lost, there will be no remainder. Also, you should be aware that no rounding of the result is performed. This means that positive numbers are truncated toward zero, and negative numbers will be truncated toward negative infinity. In other words, 5/2 will result in 2, while −5/2 will result in −3. You can verify this for yourself by writing the binary values for 5 and −5 and then shifting.

SELF-CHECK

1) What is the bit number of the high-order bit for
   a) a byte?
   b) a word?
2) Where does the bit go that is shifted off the end for a left or right shift?
3) What is the difference between a logical shift right and an arithmetic shift right?
4) Is there a difference between the SHL and SAL instructions?
5) What register can be used to specify a shift count?
6) Write an instruction to perform a logical shift right by one bit of the DL register.
7) Write the instructions necessary to shift the BX register left by 10 bits.
8) Write the instructions necessary to divide the AX register by 16, using a shift.

====

1) a) 7
   b) 15
2) Into the carry flag.
3) The logical shift right shifts a zero into the high-order bit. The arithmetic shift right shifts the sign bit into itself.
4) No, only the mnemonics.
5) Only register CL.
6) SHR DL, 1

7) MOV   CL, 10
   SHL   BX, CL ;OR SAL CAN BE USED

8) MOV   CL, 4
   SAR   AX, CL

Rotates

Rotates are very similar to shifts. We can rotate to the left or right. The difference is that rather than shift in zeros, as we do for left shifts and logical right shifts, the bit that would normally fall off the end is shifted back into the word or byte at the opposite end. The rotate left (ROL) and rotate right (ROR) instructions work as follows:

ROL

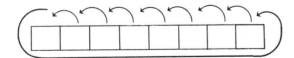

ROR

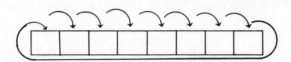

A corresponding pair of rotates, RCL and RCR, work the same as ROL and ROR except that the carry flag is included as an extra bit to the word or byte. Here is how they work:

RCL

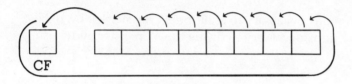

RCR

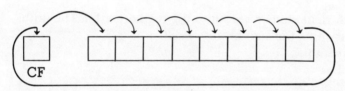

The rotate instructions have the same format as the shift instructions. You can rotate words or bytes, registers or memory variables. You can use a constant count of one or a count set up in the CL register.

The following procedure, PHEX, demonstrates the use of a rotate instruction and a logical instruction to print the contents of the AX register as a hexadecimal number.

```
;PRINT THE HEX NUMBER IN THE AX REGISTER
;
PHEX:   MOV    CX,4      ;FOUR DIGITS
OVER:   XCHG   CX,DX     ;SAVE CX IN DX
        MOV    CL,4      ;SET UP ROTATE
        ROL    AX,CL     ;ROTATE HEX DIGIT
        XCHG   CX,DX     ;RESTORE CX
        PUSH   AX        ;SAVE AX
        AND    AL,0FH    ;MASK DIGIT
        CALL   PDIG      ;PRINT AS HEX
        POP    AX        ;RESTORE AX
        LOOP   OVER      ;LOOP TILL DONE
        RET
;
PDIG    PROC
```

```
          CMP    AL,9     ;CHECK IF A—F
          JBE    PDIG1
          ADD    AL,'A'—'0'—10 ; A—F, SO FIX UP
PDIG1:    ADD    AL,'0'   ;CONVERT TO ASCII
          CALL   PUTC     ;PRINT CHARACTER
          RET
PDIG      ENDP
```

The procedure PDIG is used to convert a 4-bit hexadecimal digit to its ASCII character value. Since a hexadecimal digit can range from 0 to 9 and from A to F, a check must be made to ensure that the proper ASCII character value is selected for digits with decimal values between 10 and 15. A rotate instruction is used rather than a shift instruction, since the order in which we must output the digits is from the high-order digit first. The left rotate accomplishes this quite nicely.

SELF-CHECK

1) There are two types of left and right rotates. What is the difference?
2) Write the instruction necessary to rotate the BL register left by 1 bit, including the carry.
3) Write the instructions necessary to rotate the BX register left by 4 bits, including the carry flag.
4) Write the instructions necessary to rotate register CX right by 3 bits, not including the carry flag.
5) Consider the AX and BX registers as one combined 32-bit register, with the AX register forming the high-order bits. Write the instructions necessary to rotate this combined register right by one bit. The carry flag is not to be rotated as part of the 32-bit register pair, but it may be used in the operation.

1) One type includes the carry flag and the other type does not.
2) RCL BL, 1
3) MOV   CL, 4
   RCL   BX, CL
4) ROR   CX, 1
   ROR   CX, 1
   ROR   CX, 1
   Note that we can't place a count in CL since CL is part of CX.
5) PUSH   BX
   SHR   BX, 1   ;GET CARRY
   RCR   AX, 1
   POP   BX
   RCR   BX, 1

The TEST Instruction

The logical instructions NOT, AND, OR, and XOR all affect the flags. They all result in CF and OF being set to zero. PF, SF, and ZF are set to the appropriate value, and AF is undefined. You can use conditional jumps after executing these instructions just as you have been doing with the arithmetic instructions, such as ADD and SUB. The zero flag (ZF) is probably the most useful flag to test. One operation performed quite often is the testing of particular bits in a word or byte. To determine whether a particular bit is a one or a zero, we can use the AND instruction with the appropriate bit set in the source operand as a mask. If the result is a zero value, the bit was a zero in the destination operand. If the result is nonzero, then the bit was originally a one. The following instructions test bit two of the AL register:

```
AND   AL, 00000100B
JZ    ZVAL              ;IF BIT WAS A ZERO
.                      ;HERE IF BIT WAS A ONE
.
```

A binary constant has been used as the mask value to make clear what bit is being tested. The AND instruction works very well as a method to test bit values if we are willing to destroy the value in the destination register or variable. Wouldn't it be nice if we could perform this test *without* destroying the contents of the destination? Fortunately, the 8086/8088 provides a TEST instruction that does just that. In other words, TEST works like AND, except that the result is not stored. Neither the source nor the destination operands is changed. We could rewrite the above instructions using a TEST:

```
TEST  AL, 00000100B
JZ    ZVAL
.
.
```

You can test more than one bit at a time. If any of the bits is a one, the result will be nonzero.

```
TEST  AL, 00001111B
```

will be nonzero if any one of the four low-order bits is a one. It makes no difference what the values of the high-order four bits are.

SELF-TEST

1) What are the four logical instructions?
2) There are many more logical operations than the four that are implemented by the 8086/8088. For example, the NOR operation has the following truth table:

Operand 1

		0	1
Operand 2	0	1	0
	1	0	0

Write the instructions necessary to form the NOR operation of the AX and BX registers.

3) Write the instructions that will exchange the high-order and low-order nibbles of the AL register. (A nibble is four bits.)

4) Write the equivalent of SHR AX, 1 using only logical and rotate instructions.

5) Is SHR BX, 5 a legal instruction?

6) If we treat AX and BX as a combined 32-bit register, with AX forming the high-order 16 bits, write the instructions necessary to perform an arithmetic shift right of 3 bits.

7) Can you think of a way to perform NOT AX using another logical instruction?

8) Write an instruction that will flip the low-order bit of register BL. All other bits remain the same.

9) Write an instruction to test whether bit 12 of register AX is a one.

10) Write the instructions to test whether any of the low-order 4 bits of register DL are zero. You can destroy the contents of register DL in the process.

1) AND, OR, XOR, and NOT.

2) OR   AX, BX
   NOT   AX

3) MOV   CL, 4
   ROR   AL, CL

4) RCR   AX, 1
   AND   AX, 7FFFH

5) No, a count greater than one must be specified in the CL register.

6)
```
        MOV    CX, 3
NEXT:   SAR    AX, 1
        RCR    BX, 1
        LOOP   NEXT
```

7) XOR   AX, 0FFFFH

8) XOR BL, 01H

9) TEST   AX, 1000H

10) NOT   DL
    TEST   DL, 0FH
    JNZ   label   ;IF A BIT WAS ZERO

CHAPTER 11

String Instructions

A string is a set of consecutive bytes or words in memory. The string may run in ascending or descending order in memory. The string instructions form a group of instructions designed to manipulate strings of bytes or words rather than just a single byte or word.

The string instructions are not really needed, but they give you the ability to perform relatively complex operations with only a few instructions. Without the power of the string instructions, programs involving manipulating strings of bytes or words would be considerably longer. In addition to moving strings of bytes or words from one place in memory to another, the string instructions also allow us to scan a string for a match or mismatch of a byte or word and to compare two strings. The 80186/80188 CPU also gives us the capability to move strings to and from I/O ports.

The basic string instructions, or *primitives* as they are called, operate on a single byte or word only. Their power is enhanced by the use of special *prefix bytes* that cause the string instructions to be repeated over and over until a certain condition is met. These special prefix bytes work only with the string instructions. If we wish to repeat "any" instruction, we must use a conventional loop.

Another feature of the string instructions is that their operands are implicit and specified by pointers contained in the SI and DI registers. Remember that the SI (source index) and DI (destination index) are general purpose registers that we have been able to use all along. Their use by the string instructions is somewhat special. If a string instruction requires a source and/or destination operand, the operand must come from a location pointed to by these respective registers. Also, the source string comes from the data segment, and the destination string goes to the extra segment. It is possible to override the source segment with a segment override prefix, but not the destination segment. This must *always* be the extra segment.

Moving Strings

The first string instruction we will discuss is the move string instruction (MOVS). The general form of MOVS is

MOVS   destination_string,source_string

This instruction will move a single byte or word from the source address to the destination address. These addresses are specified by the current values (as pointers) in the SI and DI registers. The source comes from the data segment, and the destination is in the extra segment. Since the source and destination operands are always specified by SI and DI, why must source and destination operands be specified with the instruction mnemonic? The reason is that this is the method the assembler uses to determine whether a byte move or a word move is to be performed. It is also an aid to understanding how the program works when the actual variable names of the strings are used.

The following instruction will move a single byte from STR1 to STR2:

```
                MOVS      STR2,STR1
                  .
                  .
                  .
;DATA SEGMENT
STR1          DB          100 DUP(?)
;EXTRA SEGMENT
STR2          DB          100 DUP(?)
```

Naturally, this assumes that SI and DI are currently pointing to bytes contained in the strings. We can set up the SI and DI registers using the following instructions:

```
MOV   SI,OFFSET STR1
MOV   DI,OFFSET STR2
```

So far, the MOVS instruction looks pretty much like a MOV instruction except for the method used to obtain the source and destination operands. In fact, we could write

```
MOV   BYTE PTR [DI], [SI]
```

and have almost the equivalent of the MOVS instruction. The one remaining difference is that the string instructions cause the SI and/or DI registers to be incremented or decremented after their use. The registers are incremented or decremented by one or two, depending on whether a byte or a word instruction was executed. The direction flag (DF) is used to determine whether incrementing or decrementing is performed. Two instructions are used to set/clear the DF flag.

```
CLD   ;CLEAR THE DIRECTION FLAG
STD   ;SET DIRECTION FLAG
```

If the direction flag is set, then decrementing is performed. If DF is cleared, then incrementing is performed. This is equivalent to accessing strings in ascending (incrementing) or descending (decrementing) order in memory. As you can see, the power of the string instructions is becoming apparent.

All that remains is to explore the methods used to repeat the string instructions. As I have already mentioned, a special prefix byte is used to cause the string instructions to be repeated. The repeat prefix REP is used with the MOVS instruction. This prefix causes the MOVS instruction to be repeated the number of times specified by a count placed in the CX register. This count may be zero, in which case the string instruction is not executed even once. The maximum count is 65,535. To move 100 bytes from STR1 to STR2, we would write the following instructions:

```
CLD
MOV   CX,100
MOV   SI,OFFSET STR1
MOV   DI,OFFSET STR2
REP   MOVS   STR2,STR1
```

Notice that the CLD instruction is included to make sure the strings are accessed in ascending order.

Sometimes we may not know the actual symbol names for the source and destination strings. This might be the case if a string operation were performed as part of a procedure, with the operands passed as parameters to the procedure. It is perfectly legal to write the following:

```
REP MOVS     WORD PTR [DI], [SI]
```

The assembler is thus able to determine that a word move is required. (The Digital Research assembler requires this form.)

SELF-CHECK
1) What is a string?
2) How many bytes or words does a string primitive operate on?
3) How are the source and destination operands of a string instruction obtained?
4) From what segments do the source and destination operands come?
5) How do we specify whether a string is ascending or descending?
6) What register is used to hold the count when a string is repeated?
7) Write the instructions necessary to move a 20-word ascending string named DB1 to a string named DB2. DB1 is in the data segment, and DB2 is in the extra segment.
8) Repeat Question 7 for a descending string of bytes.

======

1) A string is a set of consecutive bytes or words in memory. Strings may be ascending or descending.
2) A string primitive operates on only a single byte or word. Repeat prefixes must be used with a string primitive to cause the primitive to be repeated.
3) The source is obtained from an offset specified by the contents of the SI register. The destination is obtained from an offset specified by the contents of the DI register.

4) The source is in the data segment, and the destination is in the extra segment.

5) The direction flag (DF) is used to determine whether a string is ascending or descending. If DF is zero, the string is ascending; if DF is one, the string is descending.

6) CX.

7)
```
            CLD
            MOV      SI, OFFSET DB1
            MOV      DI, OFFSET DB2
            MOV      CX, 20
            REP MOVS DB2, DB1
            .
            .
            .
;DATA SEG
DB1         DW       20 DUP(?)
;EXTRA SEG
DB2         DW       20 DUP(?)
```

8)
```
            STD
            MOV      SI, OFFSET DB1
            MOV      DI, OFFSET DB2
            MOV      CX, 20
            REP MOVS DB2, DB1
            .
            .
            .
;DATA SEG
            DB       19DUP(?)
DB1         DB       ?
;EXTRA SEG
            DB       19DUP(?)
DB2         DB       ?
```

Comparing Strings

Another powerful string instruction is the compare strings instruction (CMPS), an instruction very similar to the CMP instruction. However, like the MOVS instruction, SI and DI are used to obtain the source and destination operands. We can compare byte strings or word strings. Since the CMPS instruction will compare only two bytes or two words, we normally use an appropriate repeat prefix. We are usually interested in determining the match of two strings or substrings. The repeat prefix, REPE/REPZ (repeat while equal/repeat while zero), is provided for just this purpose. The two mnemonics refer to the same prefix, and either one can be used. Remember that in a compare operation, the operands are subtracted. Therefore, when we have equality, the result is zero.

The REPE/REPZ prefix also uses the CX register in a manner similar to the REP prefix. (The REP and REPE/REPZ prefix bytes are actually identical. Their function differs when used with different string instructions.) If we use the REPE/REPZ prefix, the CMPS instruction will be repeated so long as the bytes or words being compared are equal *and* CX is not zero. The CX register is normally initialized to the length of the strings. If we are comparing two strings of different lengths, we would set CX equal to the length of the shorter string. We would then compare the shorter string with a substring of the longer string that is equal to the length of the shorter string.

The following would compare two strings of length 25:

```
MOV   CX,25
MOV   SI,OFFSET S1
MOV   DI,OFFSET S2
CLD
REPE CMPS S2,S1
```

How do we know whether the strings were equal? The repeated CMPS instruction will terminate if either CX becomes zero or if the zero flag (ZF) becomes zero. It is best to check ZF since the strings may be equal except for the last byte or word. In this case, both ZF and CX would be zero. If we follow the above code with a JE or JNE instruction, we can jump on equal strings or not equal strings.

```
MOV   CX,25
MOV   SI,OFFSET S1
MOV   DI,OFFSET S2
CLD
REPE CMPS S2,S1
JE    MATCH            ;STRINGS MATCH
  .                    ;STRINGS DON'T MATCH
  .
```

Although it is not likely that you would want to do it, we could compare two strings for a *complete* mismatch. This would mean that we wanted every pair of bytes or words to be different. The prefix byte REPNE/REPNZ is identical to REPE/REPZ, except that the repeat is performed if the zero flag is a 1 rather than a 0. A final test of ZF would determine the success or failure of the comparison. In this case, a JNE would be used to detect that the strings were completely mismatched.

If the two strings we are comparing do not match, at the point the comparison fails, the contents of the SI and DI registers will indicate the location of the source and destination bytes or words immediately following the pair that failed to match. The contents of CX will indicate the remaining length of the strings.

What if it is not convenient to have the destination string in the extra segment or the source string in the data segment? Suppose we want to compare two strings in the data segment. We can fool the string instructions by setting the ES register to the value contained in the DS register. If the current value in the ES register is important, we can save and restore it; otherwise the following instructions are all that are needed:

```
MOV   AX,DS
MOV   ES,AX
```

Another way to do this is as follows:

```
PUSH   DS
POP    ES
```

We have to be careful that we reference the destination operand by register indirect addressing, [DI], and not by the name of the variable. If we want to use the variable name, we must be sure to add an ASSUME directive. In that case, we can load the ES register directly from the segment name.

```
MOV      AX, segname
MOV      ES, AX
ASSUME   ES:segname
```

If we try to use a variable name that is not in the segment indicated by the last ASSUME for the ES register, the assembler will generate an error because it thinks that you can't reach that variable with the current ES register. Since no variable name is used with register indirect addressing, the assembler assumes that you know what you are doing.

As I mentioned earlier, it is possible to override the source segment with an override prefix. *This is not a recommended practice.* The reason is a bit complicated. Since we normally use a repeat prefix byte with the string instructions, a segment override prefix will generate an additional prefix byte. If an interrupt should occur, the instruction will not be restarted correctly after the interrupt is processed. This is because only one of the prefix bytes will be processed. The other will be ignored. We will discuss interrupts in Chapter 13.

SELF-CHECK

1) What repeat prefixes can be used with the CMPS instruction?
2) Under what conditions can we compare strings of differing lengths?
3) Write the instructions necessary to determine whether the ascending string ALPHA is equal to the ASCII string "TRYTHISONE".
4) Modify the program of Question 3 to output the character in ALPHA that caused a mismatch if one occurred.
5) What do we have to do if the destination string is not in the current extra segment?

---

1) REPE/REPZ or REPNE/REPNZ
2) If the count is set to the size of the smaller string, we can check whether the smaller string is a substring of the larger. We must be sure that the strings overlap.
3)
```
       MOV      CX, 10
       MOV      SI, OFFSET S1
       MOV      DI, OFFSET ALPHA
       CLD
       REPE CMPS ALPHA, S1
```
(continued on next page)

```
              JE        MATCH
              .
              .
;DATA SEGMENT
S1      DB        'TRYTHISONE'
;EXTRA SEGMENT
ALPHA   DB        10 DUP(?)
4)            MOV       CX, 10
              MOV       SI, OFFSET S1
              MOV       DI, OFFSET ALPHA
              CLD
              REPE CMPS ALPHA, S1
              JE        MATCH
              DEC       DI
              MOV       AL, [DI]
              CALL      PUTC
              .
              .
;DATA SEGMENT
S1      DB        'TRYTHISONE'
;EXTRA SEGMENT
ALPHA   DB        10 DUP(?)
```

5) We must set the extra segment base register to the segment containing the destination operand. This can be done by the following:

```
MOV      AX, segname
MOV      ES, AX
ASSUME   ES:segname
```

where segname is the name of the segment containing the destination operand.

Scanning Strings

The scan string instruction (SCAS) is almost identical in operation to the
compare string instruction, except that the source operand is taken from the
AL or AX register, rather than from the location pointed to by the SI register.
Only the DI register is automatically updated. We can use the SCAS
instruction to scan a string for the first match or mismatch of the byte or
word in AL or AX. Suppose we wish to find the first nonblank character in a
character string. The following instructions would do this:

```
MOV   AL,32    ;ASCII CODE FOR BLANK
MOV   DI,OFFSET CSTRING
MOV   CX,25    ;25 CHAR STRING
CLD
REPE SCAS BYTE PTR [DI]
DEC   DI
```

After these instructions are executed, the DI register will point to the first
nonblank character, or to the byte immediately following the string if all the

bytes of the string were blank. In the latter case, the CX register would be 0. Otherwise, the CX register indicates the number of characters remaining in the string.

We can also use the SCAS instruction to find the first occurrence of a particular byte or word. Suppose we want to find the first word of a word string that is equal to 0. Here's how we do it:

```
MOV   AX,0
MOV   DI,OFFSET WSRING
MOV   CX, 100  ;100 WORDS
CLD
REPNE SCAS WORD PTR [DI]
SUB   DI,2
```

Notice that we subtracted two from the DI register since we were scanning a word string.

Two additional string instructions are provided. They are complementary. The load string (LODS) and the store string (STOS) instructions move a byte or a word to or from the AL or AX register. Their general form is:

```
LODS   source_string
STOS   destination_string
```

The SI register is used to obtain the location of the source string, and the DI register is used to obtain the location of the destination string. Both instructions may be used with a repeat prefix, but it makes sense only for the STOS instruction. If the LODS instruction is repeated, it will repeatedly overwrite the contents of AL or AX. The STOS instruction can be used to store a constant value in every element of a string. The following instructions will store an ASCII blank in each element of the string:

```
CLD
MOV   CX,string_length
MOV   DI,OFFSET STRING
MOV   AL,32  ;ASCII CODE FOR BLANK
REP STOS STRING
```

Neither the LODS nor the STOS instructions affects the flag registers. Therefore it is not possible to use a repeat prefix other than REP. LODS and STOS can be used together in a normal loop if we wish to modify the elements of a string. The following instructions add the constant 1 to every element of a string:

```
          CLD
          MOV   AX,DS
          MOV   ES,AX
          MOV   CX,string_length
          MOV   SI,OFFSET STRING
          MOV   DI,OFFSET STRING
NEXT:     LODS  WORD PTR [SI]
```

(continued on next page)

```
        ADD    AX,1
        STOS   WORD PTR [DI]
        LOOP   NEXT
```

Naturally, more complicated loops can be written that are built up of the string primitives.

As a final example, the following instructions will search STR1 for the substring STR2. STR2 is smaller than STR1.

```
        CLD
        MOV    CX,COUNT
        MOV    BX,OFFSET STR1
NEXT:   MOV    DI,BX
        MOV    SI,OFFSET STR2
        PUSH   CX
        MOV    CX,L2
        REP CMPS STR1,STR2
        POP    CX
        JE     MATCH   ;JUMP ON A MATCH
        INC    BX
        LOOP   NEXT
        .               ;HERE ON NO MATCH
        .
        .

;EXTRA SEGMENT
L1      EQU    length_of_STR1
STR1    DB     L1 DUP (?)
;DATA SEGMENT
L2      EQU    length_of_STR2
STR2    DB     L2 DUP (?)
COUNT   EQU    L1-L2+1
```

COUNT is equal to the length of STR1 minus the length of STR2 plus one. For example, if STR1 is 100 bytes long and STR2 is 5 bytes, COUNT would equal 96. If the strings are not fixed length, then L1, L2, and COUNT would have to be variables and be set up by your program. These instructions assume that the string we are searching is in the extra segment, and that the substring is in the data segment. PUSH and POP are used to save and restore the CX register so that the LOOP instruction will operate properly.

SELF-TEST

1) Why do we specify the operands of a string instruction if they always come from the offsets in the SI and DI registers?
2) Is there any way to override the default segments of a string instruction?
3) What repeat prefixes are used with what string instructions?
4) Write the instructions necessary to find the first occurrence of the value 1234H in an ascending word table at location DATTBL. Print

the entry number in the table. The first entry is 1, and the table contains 100 entries. Don't print anything if there is no match.

5) Write the instructions necessary to clear a 100-byte ascending string at BETA.

1) To provide the information necessary for the assembler to generate the proper byte or word instruction. Additionally, this makes it easier to understand what the program is doing.

2) We can use a segment override prefix on the source operand only. The destination will always come from the extra segment. It is not a recommended practice to use a segment override prefix. The best approach is to load the segment base registers, and then use the appropriate ASSUME directives.

3) REP is used with MOVS and STOS. REPE/REPZ and REPNE/REPNZ are used with the CMPS and SCAS instructions. LODS is not used with a repeat prefix.

4)
```
        CLD
        MOV    DI, OFFSET DATTBL
        MOV    AX, 1234H
        MOV    CX, 100
        REPNE  SCAS  DATTBL
        JNE    NOMATCH
        MOV    AX, 100
        SUB    AX, CX
        CALL   OUTDEC
        CALL   NEWLINE
NOMATCH:.

;EXTRA SEGMENT
DATTBL  DW     100 DUP(?)
```

5)
```
        MOV    CX, 100
        MOV    DI, OFFSET BETA
        CLD
        MOV    AL, 0
        STOS   BETA

;EXTRA SEGMENT
BETA    DB     100 DUP(?)
```

Advanced Arithmetic

In Chapters 4 and 5 you learned the ADD, SUB, INC, and DEC instructions. These instructions, along with the flags register, give us the capability to perform other arithmetic operations, such as multiplication and division. For example, we can perform multiplication by repeated addition. Division can be performed by repeated subtraction. These are not the best methods to use, but they are simple. If we also use the shift instructions you learned in Chapter 10, more efficient algorithms can be implemented. Fortunately the 8086/8088 has a set of powerful arithmetic instructions that include multiplication and division, as well as some other rather interesting instructions. In this chapter we will take a look at the complete set of arithmetic instructions and introduce some new concepts, such as decimal arithmetic. Yes, "decimal" arithmetic. Up to this point we have dealt strictly with binary arithmetic operations. If you are curious, read on.

Multiple Precision Addition and Subtraction

Before we discuss the multiplication and division instructions, I want to introduce the concept of arithmetic *precision*. Basically, the precision of a calculation is proportional to the number of bits used in the calculation. The more bits we use, the greater the precision. Even though we are confined to integer arithmetic, a larger number of bits allow us to represent larger numbers. These larger numbers can represent *scaled* values. For example, we can represent time intervals in thousandths of seconds rather than in seconds. This requires the ability to represent numbers 1,000 times larger than the equivalent times in seconds. However, the precision is greater since all our times would be stored with accuracy down to a thousandth of a second.

The 8086/8088 performs additions and subtractions on bytes or words. Therefore, there are actually two built-in precisions available. What if 16 bits do not constitute a large enough precision for our calculations? Is there anything we can do? The answer is yes, but not with a single instruction. We can perform multiple precision operations by representing our numbers as multiple numbers of bytes or words. Normally it would make no sense to represent numbers as two bytes rather than a word. However, three bytes, two words, or other higher multiples of bytes or words are logical.

How do we store multiple precision values in memory? You may recall that single words are stored in memory with the low-order (least significant) byte coming first. We can adhere to this convention and require multiple precision numbers to be stored with the lowest-order bytes or words coming first. This is not absolutely necessary, but it keeps things consistent. For example, if we have a double-word value, 12345678H, it can be stored as:

```
V1   DW   5678H
V2   DW   1234H
```

The assembler automatically reverses the bytes for the two bytes of each DW directive.

Suppose we want to add two double-precision integers, A and B, and store the result in variable C? We will assume that all three variables are stored low-order bytes first. The following directives might be used to reserve storage:

```
A   DW   2 DUP(?)
B   DW   2 DUP(?)
C   DW   2 DUP(?)
```

Adding the two low-order bytes is straightforward:

```
MOV   AX,A
ADD   AX,B
```

The result is now in the AX register. We can store this result as the low-order word of C:

```
MOV   C,AX
```

You might be tempted to say that all we have to do is repeat the above instructions for the two high-order words of A and B. This is almost correct, except for the fact that we might have had a carry from the low-order addition. This carry must be added to the calculation for the high-order words. The carry flag (CF) is set/reset as a result of our first addition. All we have to do is add the carry flag to our high-order addition. The add with carry instruction (ADC) will do this automatically. The remaining instructions are:

```
MOV   AX,A+2
ADC   AX,B+2
MOV   C+2,AX
```

Notice that the addresses of the high-order words are A+2, B+2, and C+2. Two bytes must be accounted for in advancing to the next word address. We can use the above procedure to add numbers of any precision. We use an ADD instruction for the lowest-order byte or word, and all other additions are performed with the ADC instruction.

Multiple precision subtraction can be performed in a similar manner, using the SUB instruction and the subtract with borrow instruction (SBB).

The following instructions will subtract the three-byte variable A from B and store the result in C:

```
MOV   AL,B
SUB   AL,A
MOV   C,AL
MOV   AL,B+1
SBB   AL,A+1
MOV   C+1,AL
MOV   AL,B+2
SBB   AL,A+2
MOV   C+2,AL
        .
        .
;DATA SEGMENT
A        DB      3 DUP(?)
B        DB      3 DUP(?)
C        DB      3 DUP(?)
```

SELF-CHECK

1) What is meant by arithmetic precision?
2) You have a requirement to store monetary values from 0 to 1 billion dollars down to the nearest penny. What scaling is required, and what precision is needed to store these values?
3) How are multiple precision values stored in memory?
4) Set up the value 100,000 decimal as a multiple precision number consisting of 3 bytes.
5) Write the instructions necessary to add the constant of Problem 4 to the 3-byte variable ALPHA.

---

1) Arithmetic precision refers to the number of bytes or words that are used to represent a numeric value.
2) One billion is 1,000,000,000. If we scale by two decimal digits to include pennies, we must be able to accommodate numbers as large as 100,000,000,000. This requires 5 bytes.
3) In consecutive memory locations, with the low-order bytes first.
4) We must first convert this number to the hexadecimal value 186A0H. This can be placed in memory as

```
CONST   DB   0A0H
        DB   086H
        DB   001H
```

```
5) MOV   AL, ALPHA
   ADD   AL, CONST
   MOV   ALPHA, AL
   MOV   AL, ALPHA+1
   ADC   AL, CONST+1
   MOV   ALPHA+1, AL
```

```
MOV   AL, ALPHA+2
ADC   AL, CONST+2
MOV   ALPHA+2, AL
```

Multiplication and Division

The 8086/8088 has two multiply and two divide instructions. One pair of multiply and divide instructions is used for unsigned values; the other pair is used for signed values. Unlike addition and subtraction, signed and unsigned multiplies and divides require you to use different instructions. The four instructions are:

MUL   unsigned multiply
IMUL   signed multiply
DIV   unsigned divide
IDIV   signed divide

We will discuss multiplication first. A property of the multiplication of two numbers of a given precision is that the result of the multiplication can have a precision equal to the sum of the precisions of the two numbers. This means that if we multiply two bytes, we can have a result up to two bytes or one word in length. If we multiply two words, we can have a result up to four bytes or two words in length.

The MUL and IMUL instructions both have a single operand. This can be a byte or a word from memory, or a register. Each instruction multiplies the byte or word in AL or AX by the source operand. If the source operand is a byte, then AL is multiplied by the operand, and the result is placed in AX. The low-order byte of the result is in AL, and the high-order byte of the result is placed in AH. If the source operand is a word, then AX is multiplied by the source operand, and the result is placed in the register pair AX, DX. The low-order word of the result is placed in AX, and the high-order word of the result is placed in DX. In both cases the CF and OF flags are set if the high-order byte or word is nonzero. This allows us to check whether or not our result has exceeded single precision.

The following instructions multiply the two bytes contained in registers BH and BL:

```
MOV   AL,BH
MUL   BL
```

The result is in AX. The following instructions multiply word variables X and Y:

```
MOV   AX,X
MUL   Y
```

The result is in the register pair, AX, DX. The following instructions multiply the AX register by 100:

```
MOV   BX,100
MUL   BX
```

It is important to note that we cannot multiply by an immediate oper-
and, nor can we multiply AX by a byte register, even though the constant
100 will fit into a byte register. If the second instruction had been

```
MUL   BL
```

the AL register would have been multiplied by 100, but not the AX register.

The IMUL instruction works exactly the same as the MUL instruction,
except that signed numbers are used. This means that the word or double
word result will have the sign bit of the result extended through all the
high-order bits. If the result is negative, the high-order byte or word (AH or
DX) will not be zero even if there are no significant digits present. CF and OF
are set only if there are significant digits present in the high-order byte or
word.

SELF-CHECK

1) What are the multiplication and division instructions used with
   a) unsigned arithmetic?
   b) signed arithmetic?
2) What is the precision of the result of a multiplication?
3) Write the instructions necessary to multiply the AX register by 10.
   Use signed arithmetic.
4) Write the instructions necessary to multiply the AL register by the
   DL register. Save the result in a word variable named COUNT. Use
   unsigned arithmetic.

---

1) a) MUL and DIV
   b) IMUL and IDIV
2) The precision of the result is equal to the sum of the precisions of
   the numbers being multiplied.
3) ```
   MOV   BX,10
   IMUL  BX
   ```
4) ```
   MUL   DL
   MOV   COUNT, AX
   ```

Division is essentially the inverse of multiplication. For unsigned divisions, we use the divide instruction (DIV). If the source operand is a byte, it
is divided into the 2 byte dividend, which is placed in the AX register. The
divide operation produces a single-byte quotient in the AL register, and a
single-byte remainder in the AH register. If the source operand is a word, it is
divided into the double-word value contained in the register pair, AX and DX.

DX contains the high-order word. The single-word quotient is placed in the AX register, and the single-word remainder in the DX register.

The following instructions will divide the single word in AX by the constant 10:

```
MOV   BX,10   ;DIVIDE BY 10
MOV   DX,0
DIV   BX
```

The integer part of the result is in the AX register. Notice that we placed a zero in the DX register. This is necessary if we are dividing a single-precision word value. Otherwise, the double-precision word value, consisting of the AX and DX pair, would be used. We must also remember to perform a similar operation when we divide a single-precision byte in the AL register. In this case, we clear the AH register:

```
MOV   BL,25   ;DIVIDE BY 25
MOV   AH,0
DIV   BL
```

Performing signed division is almost as simple. The only difference is that if we have a single-precision byte or word dividend, we must sign-extend to the high-order byte or word. Simply zeroing the byte or word is incorrect. As is to be expected with the power of the 8086/8088, there are special instructions for doing this. To sign-extend the byte in AL to the AH register, we would use the convert byte to word instruction (CBW). The use of this instruction is not restricted to division. It can be used anytime we have a signed byte in AL and need a signed word of equal value in AX. Similarly, the convert word to double word (CWD) instruction sign-extends AX into DX. To perform a signed division of the word in AX, we would write the following instructions:

```
MOV   BX,10   ;DIVIDE BY 10
CWD
IDIV   BX
```

Before we leave division, there are a few more loose ends. For signed division, the sign of the remainder is always the same as that of the dividend. This means that if we divide two negative numbers, even though the quotient is positive, any remainder will be negative. If we divide −23 by −10, the execution of the IDIV instruction will give us a quotient of +2 in register AX and a remainder of −3 in register DX.

When we perform a division, signed or unsigned, it is possible for the quotient to be larger than the register can hold. This is always the case when we try to divide by zero. If we perform a double-precision division, word or double-word, we must be especially careful. This *overflow* condition can now occur for divisors other than zero. The overflow flag (OF) is not used to detect this situation. Instead, a special software interrupt is generated. Interrupt type 0 is reserved for this condition. The result of such a division leaves an undefined result. If you want to ensure an error-free program, you may wish to use interrupt type 0 to "trap" your program. We will discuss interrupts in the next chapter, and you will then know how they can be utilized.

---

1) Where is the dividend placed if we have a byte divisor?
2) Where is the dividend placed if we have a word divisor?
3) Write the instructions necessary to divide the unsigned value in register AL by a byte variable named SCALE.
4) Repeat Problem 3 for a signed value.

1) In the AX register. AH contains the high-order byte.
2) In the AX and DX pair. DX contains the high-order bytes.
3) MOV   AH, 0
   DIV   SCALE
4) CBW
   IDIV SCALE

Decimal Arithmetic

Up to this point, all our numerical values have been represented as binary data consisting of one or more bytes. When we input decimal numbers to a program, they must be converted to binary. Similarly, when we want to output a decimal number, it must be converted from the internal binary representation. The INDEC and OUTDEC procedures introduced in Chapter 4 perform these operations. As it turns out, the 8086/8088 has a number of instructions that let us represent decimal numbers internally in a way that makes the input and output conversions much simpler. This representation is called binary coded decimal, or BCD.

It requires four bits to represent the digits 0 through 9. As you may recall, we can actually count up to 15 with four bits. That, of course, allows us hexadecimal representation. If, however, we restrict the values of a group of four bits to range from 0 through 9, we can represent a decimal number as a set of these 4-bit groups. These half bytes are sometimes called *nibbles*. There are two nibbles per byte, and four nibbles per word. This allows us to represent up to two decimal digits per byte, or four decimal digits per word. The decimal number 35 can be written in BCD form as 00110101_2. The two decimal digits are contained in one byte. Note that this number would be 53_{10} if the binary value were converted to decimal.

We can also represent decimal numbers in BCD, using only the low-order nibble of each byte. The high-order nibble is set at zero. There are advantages in doing this, even though it takes more storage to hold our decimal numbers. When we store two decimal digits per byte, our representation is technically known as *packed BCD*. When we store only one decimal digit per byte, the representation is known as *unpacked BCD* and, less popu-larly, as *ASCII*. This latter designation is not strictly correct, as you will recall from Chapter 1. The ASCII values for the decimal digits 0 through 9 are 48_{10} through 57_{10}. However, a conversion merely requires adding 48_{10} to our unpacked BCD value to yield a correct ASCII character. On input we subtract 48_{10} to obtain the correct unpacked BCD value.

So far so good, but how do we use packed and unpacked BCD values in performing arithmetic? If we have to convert them to pure binary, we have not gained anything. The answer lies in examining what happens when we perform additions, subtractions, multiplications, and divisions of BCD numbers. Suppose we add the unpacked BCD numbers 2 and 7. In the binary representation, these numbers are 00000010_2 and 00000111_2. Adding them by using the ADD instruction would yield 00001001_2, or 9 decimal. This is just what we want. However, suppose we add 5 and 7. Our result will now be 00001100_2. This is not a valid packed or unpacked BCD number, since the low-order nibble is greater than 9. The problem gets worse if we add 8 and 9. This gives us 00010001_2. We might interpret this as 11_{10} if we were using packed BCD. This is still not right. What we really want is for the low-order nibble to be set to the correct BCD value and somehow to determine whether we have a carry to the high-order nibble. In other words, we really wanted 00000010_2 when we added 5 and 7, and 00000111_2 when we added 8 and 9. In both these cases, we have a carry corresponding to 10_{10}.

The above problem is solved by the use of a number of instructions designed to correct an arithmetic operation after it has been performed. These instructions fix up the low-order nibble and set the carry flag when appropriate. The instructions are:

AAA   ASCII Adjust for Addition
AAS   ASCII Adjust for Subtraction
AAM   ASCII Adjust for Multiplication
AAD   ASCII Adjust for Division

AAA and AAS assume that an addition or subtraction has been per-formed, with the result left in the AL register. The following will add two variables, V1 and V2, and will perform the proper adjustment:

```
MOV    AL,V1
ADD    AL,V2
AAA
```

V1 and V2 would have to be valid unpacked BCD numbers. The instruc-tions for subtraction are similar except that the AAS instruction is used. If we multiply two unpacked BCD numbers, we get a result ranging from 0 to 81_{10}. If we use the AAM instruction to correct a multiplication in which the result is in AH and AL, we get two valid unpacked BCD numbers, the high-order digit in AH and the low-order digit in AL. There is never a carry since two unpacked BCD digits are large enough to contain our greatest result. Here is how we multiply V1 and V2 and correct the result:

```
MOV   AL,V1
MUL   V2
AAM
```

Division is almost as simple. However, there is one difference. We must correct *before* we perform the division. Remember that a division uses a double-precision value; it produces a single-precision integer quotient and a single-precision remainder. Two unpacked BCD values are used as the dividend, the high-order digit in AH and the low-order digit in AL. To make things clearer, let's use some constants rather than variables. If we want to divide 25_{10} by 5_{10}, we perform the following:

```
MOV   AH,2
MOV   AL,5
MOV   BL,5
AAD
DIV   BL
```

These instructions would result in the unpacked BCD digits 5 in AL and 0 in AH.

Now that we know how to perform additions, subtractions, multiplications, and divisions of unpacked BCD values, we can extend these operations to multidigit decimal numbers. Suppose we are storing 10-digit decimal numbers as arrays of bytes. If the first entry in the array corresponds to the low-order byte, we can add two of these numbers with the following instructions:

```
        CLC
        MOV   CX,10
        MOV   BX,0
NEXT:   MOV   AL,N1[BX]
        ADC   AL,N2[BX]
        AAA
        MOV   N3[BX],AL
        INC   BX
        LOOP  NEXT
```

In this example the two decimal numbers, N1 and N2, are added together, with the result stored in N3. The BX register is used as an index into the arrays for each decimal number. The CLC instruction is used to clear the carry flag prior to the first add with carry. If we don't make sure the carry flag is initially clear, we might get an erroneous result.

If we want to output the unpacked BCD array N3, we can use the following instructions:

```
        MOV   CX,10
        MOV   BX,9
OVER:   MOV   AL,N3[BX]
        ADD   AL,48
        CALL  PUTC
        DEC   BX
        LOOP  OVER
```

Note that the index in BX runs from 9 to 0. This is because we must output the decimal number with the high-order digit first.

Write the instructions to input an 8-digit unpacked BCD number into an array N.

```
        MOV    CX,8
        MOV    BX,7
OVER:   CALL   GETC
        SUB    AL,48
        MOV    N[BX],AL
        DEC    BX
        LOOP   OVER
```

These instructions assume that you enter a valid decimal number exactly 8 digits long. The high-order digits are entered first.

We can perform subtraction of multidigit unpacked BCD numbers in a similar manner. The subtract with borrow instruction (SBB) must be used. Multiplication and division are not as simple. It is possible to perform multiplication with the same technique we use when performing this operation by hand. When we multiply by hand, we are actually multiplying individual decimal digits, shifting and adding. We can do all of these things with the unpacked BCD instructions. Shifting to the next decimal digit position involves merely adding one to the array index. Division is more difficult. Those readers who are interested in performing multiple precision multiplication and division should refer to one of the many texts on numerical methods for computers. Coverage of these techniques is beyond the scope of this book.

Before we leave our discussion of decimal arithmetic, there are two additional 8086/8088 instructions that we can use with packed BCD numbers. Remember that a packed BCD number is one in which two BCD digits are stored in a single byte. We can add and subtract these numbers just as we did with unpacked BCD numbers. However, the instructions AAA and AAS will not correctly adjust the results. The following instructions are provided for packed BCD addition and subtraction:

DAA   Decimal Adjust for Addition
DAS   Decimal Adjust for Subtraction

When we input or output a packed BCD number, we must remember to unpack the number for output and pack the number for input. We can output a single byte of a packed BCD number with the following:

```
PUSH  AX
MOV   CL,4
SHR   AL,CL
ADD   AL,48
CALL  PUTC
POP   AX
AND   AL,0FH
ADD   AL,48
CALL  PUTC
```

To perform additions and subtractions on packed BCD numbers, the high-order digit must be in the high-order four bits of the byte. The previous instructions output the byte with the high-order digit first.

The following instructions are necessary to input a single-packed BCD byte into AL:

```
CALL  GETC
SUB   AL,48
MOV   CL,4
SHL   AL,CL
MOV   BL,AL
CALL  GETC
SUB   AL,48
OR    AL,BL
```

SELF-TEST

1) What two arithmetic precisions are built-in to the 8086/8088 instruction set?
2) Why would it not be proper to use the CWD or CBW instructions with unsigned arithmetic?
3) What is the sign of the remainder in signed division?
4) What is the difference between packed and unpacked BCD?
5) Write the instructions necessary to subtract the 2-byte unpacked BCD number at N1 from the 2-byte unpacked BCD number at N2.
6) Why would it not be appropriate to use the IDIV instruction when dividing two unpacked BCD numbers?
7) If we perform addition and subtraction of packed BCD numbers, what instructions must we use for adjustment?
8) Write the instructions necessary to add the four packed BCD bytes at ALPHA to the four packed BCD bytes at BETA.

---

1) 8 bits for byte arithmetic, and 16 bits for word arithmetic.
2) CWD or CBW will extend the sign bit. If the sign bit happens to be a one, the wrong number will result.
3) The sign of the dividend.
4) In unpacked BCD, the high-order 4 bits, or nibble, of each byte are 0. A single BCD value is present in the low-order nibble. In packed BCD,

a BCD value is present in both the high-order and the low-order nibble.

5)
```
MOV   AL, N2
SUB   AL, N1
AAS
MOV   N2, AL
MOV   AL, N2+1
SBC   AL, N1+1
MOV   N2+1, AL
```

6) Unpacked BCD numbers are not signed. IDIV is used for binary signed arithmetic.

7) DAA for adjusting an addition, and DAS for adjusting a subtraction.

8)
```
         MOV    CX, 4
         MOV    BX, 0
         CLC
NEXT:    MOV    AL, BETA[BX]
         ADC    AL, ALPHA[BX]
         DAA
         MOV    BETA[BX], AL
         INC    BX
         LOOP   NEXT
```

Input/Output and
Miscellaneous Instructions

If you are a beginning assembly language programmer, you will probably not want to do your own input and output. In fact, even advanced assembly language programmers normally let the operating system do this job for them. The main reason is that input/output is dependent on the particular hardware configuration of your computer. In order to allow the greatest transportability of programs, it is desirable to keep direct input/output to a minimum. However, in order to make this book as complete as possible, we will briefly discuss the 8086/8088 input/output instructions.

It may come as a surprise, but the 8086/8088 has only two instructions for input and output. (The 80186, 80188, and 80286 have four.) These two instructions have the appropriate mnemonics IN and OUT. Before we discuss the details of these two instructions, let's examine how input and output devices are connected to the CPU.

Each input or output device requires a hardware interface to the CPU chip. More sophisticated interfaces are known as controllers. For example, you probably have a floppy disk controller if your computer has a floppy disk. If you have an external CRT terminal, it will be connected via a serial data interface. These interfaces and controllers are connected to the CPU in such a way that the CPU can exchange bytes or words of information using the IN and OUT instructions. This information can represent control, status, or data. Control information is output to the interface, telling the interface what we would like it to do. For example, we might instruct our floppy disk controller to initiate the reading of a particular record of data. Status information is input from the interface to tell us the current state of the interface. This information might inform us of any errors encountered during a previous operation.

Data is either input from or output to the interface, and interpretation depends on the type of input/output device. A CRT terminal would naturally expect the data to be ASCII character codes, not the binary representation of numeric information. Some I/O interfaces have the added ability to transfer data directly to or from memory. This technique is called DMA, which stands for direct memory access.

The IN and OUT instructions are similar to a MOV instruction used to transfer data between memory and a register. However, instead of the data residing in memory, it is transferred to or from input/output ports. The 8086/8088 allows up to 64K (65,536) input/output ports. A port can be used for control, status, or data. The use and allocation of ports depend on the particular interfaces and on the particular computer you are using. Before I give an example of a particular interface, let's examine the IN and OUT instructions in more detail. The general format of these instructions is:

```
IN      AL,port
OUT     port,AL
```

or

```
IN      AX,port
OUT     port,AX
```

The port is specified in one of two ways. If the port number is less than 256_{10}, it can be specified as an immediate value. If the port number is equal to or greater than 256_{10}, it must first be placed in the DX register.

We can transfer either 8 or 16 bits, depending on whether we use AL or AX. The choice depends on the particular interface in use. The AL or AX registers are the only ones we can use with the IN and OUT instructions. The following are all legal IN and OUT instructions:

```
IN      AL,20H
OUT     DX,AL
IN      AX,DX
OUT     255,AX
```

SELF-CHECK

1) What are the input/output instructions of the 8086/8088?
2) What type of information is passed between the CPU and an I/O interface or controller?
3) How many input/output ports are allowed with the 8086/8088?
4) Write the instruction necessary to output a byte to port 25.
5) Write the instructions necessary to input a word from port 1000H.

1) IN and OUT.
2) Control, status, and data.
3) 65,536
4) OUT   25, AL

5) MOV   DX, 1000H
   IN   AX, DX

Serial I/O

Many microcomputers are equipped with serial communications interfaces. Your CRT terminal or printer can be connected via a serial interface. Another popular interface is the parallel interface. The terms serial and parallel refer to the methods used to transfer data from the input/output device to the interface. A parallel interface transfers a complete byte or word at a time. A serial interface transfers a byte or word a single bit at a time. The advantage of a serial interface is that fewer wires are needed to make the connection. A parallel interface requires at least one wire for each bit. A disadvantage of a serial interface is that data cannot be transferred as rapidly as with the parallel interface.

At the heart of the serial interface is a chip commonly known as a Universal Asynchronous Receiver Transmitter (UART). Each byte of data is sent or received as a stream of bits. Two additional bits are included for each byte of data. A start bit is included to tell the UART that a byte is to follow. A stop bit is used to verify to the UART that we are finished with the current byte. Without start and stop bits, the UART would not be able to ensure *framing*. When a framing error occurs, some of the bits from one byte are mixed up with some of the bits from a previous byte. Figure 9 shows this typical asynchronous serial format. The most popular format is for 8 data bits, 1 start bit, and 1 stop bit, giving a total of 10 bits for each byte of data sent or received.

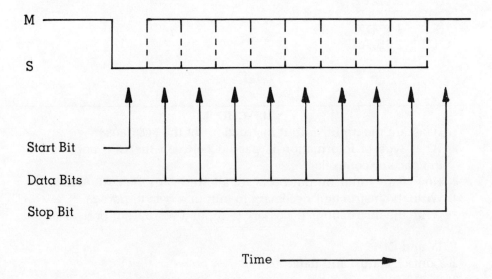

M—Marking or a logical one.
S—Spacing or a logical zero.

Figure 9. Asynchronous serial format.

If each byte is to represent an ASCII character code, we have an extra bit available. This bit can be permanently set to a one or to zero, or it may be used as a *parity bit*. A parity bit is used to help verify that the data have been received without error. The way we use a parity bit is very simple. We count the number of data bits that are ones. We include the parity bit, but not the start and stop bits. If we have an even number, we have *even* parity. If we have an odd number, we have *odd* parity. Most serial interfaces allow a programmer to specify whether even, odd, or no parity is required. The interface normally generates and/or checks the parity if we wish.

The 8086/8088 flags register includes a parity flag (PF). This flag is set to a one if we have even parity. In other words, PF is a one if there are an even number of one bits in the byte or word. Two conditional jumps can be used to test the state of the PF flag:

JNP/JPO   Jump on odd parity
JP/JPE   Jump on even parity

A simple way to test the parity is to ensure that PF is properly set by performing an OR instruction. To test the parity of the AL register, we perform:

```
OR   AL,AL
JPO          ;JUMPS IF PARITY ODD
.            ;HERE ON EVEN PARITY
.
.
```

It is not possible to cover the complete programming of every serial interface. However, they all have a number of features in common. A status bit is used to tell the programmer when a byte or character has been received. Similarly, a status bit is used to tell the programmer when it is O.K. to send another byte. As I have already mentioned, the particular ports to which control, status, and data are read or written is hardware-dependent. So are the particular bits of the status and control registers. Figure 10 shows the bits of the status register for an Intel 8251 serial interface. The complete programming of this interface requires initializing the interface and the detection and recovery of error conditions. Since our objective is to show the use of the IN and OUT instructions, I will not cover these details.

The TxRDY and RxRDY bits are the only bits in the status register that we will discuss. TxRDY, bit 0, is set if we can output a data byte. RxRDY, bit 1, is set if a data byte is ready for input. The actual data is input or output to the data port. Let us say that our data port is at 100H, and our status port is 101H. The following instructions would be used to input a byte from the 8251 to the AL register:

```
RTEST:  IN    AL,101H  ;GET STATUS BYTE
        TEST  AL,01H   ;DO WE HAVE A BYTE?
        JE    RTEST    ;NO, KEEP TRYING
        IN    AL,100H  ;YES, GET IT
```

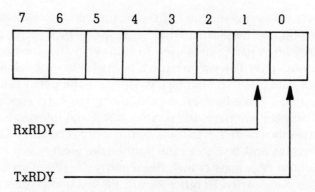

Figure 10. 8251 status register (partial).

The following instructions would output a byte from the AL register:

```
        PUSH  AX        ;SAVE OUR BYTE
TTEST:  IN    AL,101H   ;GET STATUS BYTE
        TEST  AL,02H    ;OK TO TRANSMIT?
        JE    TTEST     ;NO, TRY AGAIN
        POP   AX        ;YES, GET BYTE BACK
        OUT   100H,AL   ;OUTPUT THE BYTE
```

SELF-CHECK

1) What is the difference between a serial and a parallel interface?
2) Other than the data bits, what other bits are sent or received with a serial interface?
3) What is the parity of the following binary numbers?
   a) 11111111
   b) 10110011
   c) 00000000
   d) 11100111
4) Write the instructions necessary to jump to label ODD if the BH register contains a number with odd parity.
5) Assume that you have an 8251 serial interface at ports 0A00H for status and 0A001H for data. Write the instructions necessary to input a byte to the AL register.
6) Repeat Problem 5 for output from register AL.

---

1) A serial interface transfers data a bit at a time. A parallel interface transfers data a byte or a word at a time.
2) A start bit, stop bit, and optional parity bit.
3) a) Even parity.
   b) Odd parity.
   c) Even parity.
   d) Even parity.

```
4) OR    BH, BH
   JPO   ODD

5)         MOV    DX, 0A000H
   RTEST:  IN     AL, DX
           TEST   AL, 01H
           JE     RTEST
           INC    DX
           IN     AL, DX

6)         MOV    DX, 0A000H
           PUSH   AX
   TTEST:  IN     AL, DX
           TEST   AL, 02H
           JE     TTEST
           POP    AX
           INC    DX
           OUT    DX, AL
```

Interrupts

An advantageous feature for both microprocessors and larger computers is the interrupt mechanism. While not absolutely necessary, the mechanism has many advantages when software and hardware utilize interrupts. An interrupt is more or less what the name implies, an interruption to normal program execution. In other words, the flow of control is diverted from the normal instruction sequence.

Interrupts can be caused by software or hardware. Interrupts caused by hardware are commonly called *external* interrupts. An input/output device can be designed that will generate interrupts whenever certain events take place. Software interrupts are generated either by specific instructions or as a result of certain error conditions. For example, the 8086/8088 CPU generates an interrupt if we try to divide by zero. Before we look at the particular instructions used to generate interrupts, let's see what happens when an interrupt occurs.

Each type of interrupt has an associated type number. This number can range from 0 to 255_{10}. The first 1K bytes of memory are reserved as an *interrupt vector table*. Each interrupt type has a 4-byte entry in the interrupt vector table. Figure 11 shows how the interrupt vector table is arranged. A particular entry's address can be computed by multiplying the interrupt type number by four. Each entry consists of a code segment base address and an offset. The base address is in paragraph form, so any memory location can be specified. This segment base and the offset are interpreted as the location in memory where instructions are to be found and executed if that particular interrupt occurs. The group of instructions specified for execution when a particular interrupt occurs is called an *interrupt handler*. There is no restriction as to what these instructions may be.

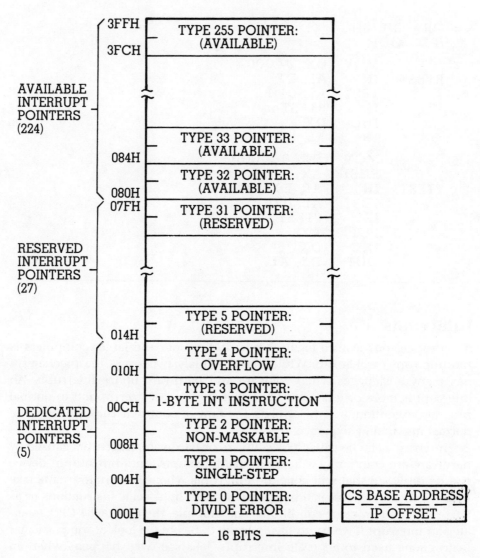

Figure 11.—Interrupt vector table. (Courtesy of Intel)

When an interrupt occurs, certain automatic events take place:

1. The flags register is pushed onto the stack.
2. The current instruction pointer is pushed onto the stack.
3. The current code segment register is pushed onto the stack.
4. External interrupts are disabled.
5. Control passes to the segment and offset obtained from the interrupt vector table.

The sequence of events that occurs when an interrupt is handled can be thought of as being very similar to a procedure call. The only difference is that the flags are saved on the stack, and interrupts are automatically disabled. In fact, we write an interrupt handler as if it were a procedure, except that a special return instruction, IRET, is used. This instruction reverses the steps that occurred when the interrupt was generated. The flags are restored from the stack, and control is returned to the instruction following the instruction that was executing when the interrupt occurred. Figure 12 shows this flow of control.

;PROGRAM IN EXECUTION

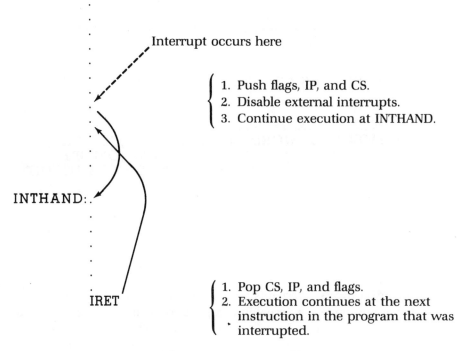

Interrupt occurs here

{
1. Push flags, IP, and CS.
2. Disable external interrupts.
3. Continue execution at INTHAND.
}

INTHAND:

{
1. Pop CS, IP, and flags.
2. Execution continues at the next instruction in the program that was interrupted.
}

IRET

Figure 12. Interrupt flow.

A software interrupt can be generated with the INT instruction. For example, if we want to generate interrupt 123_{10}, we would issue the following instruction:

INT   123

Specific interrupts of this type are quite often used to communicate with your operating system or with special programs located in read only memory (ROM). Consult your operating system manuals for the details on your particular system. Parameters can be passed by using the same techniques that we used with procedures. If you look at the instructions that are used for the standard I/O procedures in Appendix B, you can see how these procedures communicate with CP/M and MS DOS using an INT instruction.

A special instruction is used to generate an interrupt if the overflow flag (OF) is set. We can use the interrupt on overflow (INTO) instruction following an arithmetic operation. If we have an appropriate interrupt handler, it may prove useful. This handler might be used to print an error message, then abort the program. In this case, the interrupt handler would not return by using the IRET instruction. It would have to pass control to the operating system instead. The following instructions can be used to test for overflow after an addition:

```
ADD    AX,VALUE
INTO
```

The overflow interrupt is a type 4 interrupt. The following instructions could be used to set up the interrupt vector table entry for this type 4 interrupt:

```
MOV    AX,0
MOV    ES,AX    ;SET TO BASE OF INTERRUPT
                ;VECTORS
MOV    BX,4*4   ;OFFSET OF TYPE 4 INTERRUPT
MOV    AX,OFFSET INTHAND
MOV    ES:WORD PTR [BX],AX      ;SET BASE AND
                                ;OFFSET
MOV    ES:WORD PTR [BX]+2,CS    ;OF INTHAND
         .
         .
         .
INTHAND:.
         .
         .
       IRET
```

External or hardware interrupts are handled in a similar manner. A couple of instructions concern external interrupts and the flag register. A special flag bit, the interrupt enable flag (IF), is used to selectively enable or disable external interrupts. If IF is not set, external interrupts are masked. This means that if one occurs, it will not cause the normal sequence of events discussed above. We can set or clear IF with the following instructions:

```
STI    Set the interrupt enable flag
CLI    Clear the interrupt enable flag
```

Remember that IF is cleared automatically whenever *any* interrupt occurs. The IRET instruction restores the flags to their previous values. If IF is set, it will allow external interrupts to occur once again. If we want to allow external interrupts within an interrupt handler, we must issue an STI instruction.

There is one special type of external interrupt that is not affected by the IF flag: the type 2 interrupt, or nonmaskable interrupt. If your system uses this interrupt type, it will always occur. A common use of this type of interrupt is to provide interrupts for a real-time clock. We would not want to turn these interrupts off at any time, or our clock would run slow and at an unpredictable rate.

Before we leave the subject of interrupts, it should be pointed out that when control is passed to an interrupt handler, you must save and restore any registers that you use. This is just like the steps taken for procedure calls, except that the saving and restoring must be done by the interrupt handler. Also, you can't be sure that the contents of the segment base registers are what you want when you get control in an interrupt handler. If an external interrupt occurs, the segment base registers will be set to whatever segments were in use by the procedure that was interrupted. The only exception is CS. If CS were not set to the segment containing the interrupt handler code, it wouldn't have control. So you must remember to set the segment base registers to the segments you will use in the interrupt handler, then restore them to their old values prior to the interrupt return.

SELF-CHECK

1) What are the two basic types of interrupts?
2) What is the range of interrupt type numbers?
3) How many bytes are needed for each interrupt vector table entry, and what are they used for?
4) How do we find the entry in the interrupt vector table that corresponds to a particular interrupt?
5) Write the instruction necessary to generate a software interrupt of type 200.
6) Write the instructions necessary to set up the interrupt vector table for a type 100 interrupt that passes control to an interrupt handler at label COUNTUP. The interrupt handler will increment a counter variable, COUNT, in the code segment and then return.
7) Can we disable all external interrupts?

1) External or hardware interrupts and software interrupts.
2) 0 to 255.
3) Four bytes are required. They hold the segment and offset of the interrupt handler.
4) The interrupt type number is multiplied by four. This is the actual physical memory location. In other words, it is the offset into a segment with a zero paragraph address.
5) INT   200

6)
```
                MOV    AX, 0
                MOV    ES, AX
                MOV    BX, 4*100
                MOV    AX, OFFSET COUNTUP
                MOV    ES:WORD PTR [BX], AX
                MOV    ES:WORD PTR [BX]+2, CS
                .
                :
    COUNTUP:INC    COUNT
                IRET
    ;
    COUNT    DW    0
```
7) All except the nonmaskable interrupt type 2.

External Synchronization

A number of instructions are provided for special purposes. These instructions are normally not needed by the assembly language programmer, but you should be aware of their existence.

The halt instruction (HLT) will actually halt the CPU. However, external interrupts are not disabled by this instruction, and the CPU will still respond to a hardware-generated interrupt. For certain types of real-time control applications, the program is entirely driven by external interrupts. While we are waiting for one of these to occur, we can use the HLT instruction rather than an infinite loop. If you use a HLT in your program and do not have any external interrupts pending, then the only way to regain control is by resetting the CPU. This is the same procedure you follow when initially starting your operating system, or when power is first applied to your computer.

The WAIT instruction is used for testing purposes or to allow synchronization with external hardware. A special *test pin* is provided on the CPU chip. This pin is normally not used. However, if the WAIT instruction is executed, the CPU will enter a wait state until the test pin is activated. Unless your computer has a mechanism for activating this pin, the CPU will effectively halt.

The escape instruction (ESC) is provided for use with coprocessors. The 8087 numeric coprocessor is an example. This chip provides an extensive arithmetic extension to the 8086 family. (The programming of the coprocessor is covered in another Wiley book, *The 8087 Primer*, by John F. Palmer and Stephen P. Morse.) The escape instruction allows the coprocessor to receive its instructions from the 8086/8088 instruction stream. Unless a coprocessor is present, this instruction is of no use.

The LOCK instruction causes the CPU's memory bus to be locked while the next instruction is executed. This is only important for multiple processor systems. In that case, it can be used to implement a software lock. The XCHG instruction is used for that purpose. Executing

```
CHECK:   MOV    AL,1
         LOCK
         XCHG   SEM,AL
         TEST   AL,AL
         JNZ    CHECK
```

will ensure that only one processor will set the lock. The applications of such a locking mechanism can be found in most texts on operating system theory. Unless you are involved with multiple processor systems, you will never need this instruction.

An interesting instruction that doesn't fit any other place is the XLAT or translate instruction. The translate instruction takes the byte in the AL register and uses it as an offset into a table pointed to by the BX register. The value found in the table is moved into AL. This instruction can be used to translate from one character code to another, for example, from ASCII to EBCDIC. We merely load the offset of the table into BX, the character to be translated into AL, and issue the XLAT instruction. The following instructions would translate the byte value 33 to 55.

```
          MOV     BX, OFFSET TABLE
          MOV     AL, 33
          XLAT    TABLE
            .

;DATA SEGMENT
TABLE     .            ;ENTRY 0
            .

          DB 55        ;ENTRY 33
            .

            .          ;ENTRY 255
```

A pair of instructions have been provided for compatibility with the earlier 8-bit Intel 8080 and 8085 CPUs. These instructions, LAHF and SAHF, allow some of the flags to be transferred between the flags register and register AH. Only SF, ZF, AF, PF, and CF are involved. They are loaded into bits 7, 6, 4, 2, and 0, respectively, of register AH by the LAHF instruction. The SAHF instruction will load these same bits from AH back into the flag register. No other flags are affected. These instructions should not normally be used for 8086/8088 programs unless a direct conversion of an 8080/8085 program is being performed.

Last but not least of the miscellaneous instructions is the no-operation instruction (NOP). This instruction does just what its name implies, absolutely nothing. Why do most CPUs provide this instruction? It can be used as a place-holder. If you are debugging a program with a debugger, you may wish to replace one instruction by another instruction that requires fewer bytes. The extra bytes must contain a harmless instruction. The NOP is the one to use. Even though instructions like OR AL,AL don't modify any registers, the flags are affected. NOP doesn't have this side-effect. Another use of this instruction is normally invisible unless the programmer carefully examines the assembly listing. Occasionally the assembler can't predict in advance the number of bytes required for a particular instruction. It must allocate the maximum number of bytes that a particular instruction may require. If the instruction ultimately requires fewer bytes than were allocated, the extra bytes are filled with the NOP instruction.

SELF-TEST

1) Why don't most programmers do direct input/output?
2) How are input/output devices such as terminals and floppy disks connected to the CPU?
3) What registers can be used with the IN and OUT instructions?
4) What is parity?

5) What is an interrupt?
6) What is the difference between the sequence of events following an interrupt and a procedure call?
7) What are software interrupts normally used for?
8) How do we enable or disable external interrupts?
9) What will happen if an external interrupt occurs after you have executed an HLT instruction?
10) What instruction is provided to support coprocessors such as the 8087?
11) What is the purpose of the LOCK instruction?
12) Set up a table for use with the XLAT instruction that will convert the hexadecimal numbers 0 through F into the corresponding ASCII character code.

======================

1) Direct input/output is hardware- and operating system-dependent. To allow the best portability of programs, it is best to leave input/ output to the operating system.
2) I/O devices are connected to the CPU by interfaces or controllers.
3) Only AL and AX can be used for input or output. DX is used to specify port numbers greater than 255.
4) The parity of a byte or word is equivalent to whether the byte or word has an even or odd number of one bits.
5) An interrupt is a rupture in the normal flow of a program. When an interrupt occurs, control is passed to a special handler. Interrupts may be externally generated by hardware devices or generated by specific program instructions, such as the INT instruction.
6) When an interrupt occurs, the flags are saved on the stack and external interrupts are disabled. This is not done for a procedure call.
7) Software interrupts are normally used to communicate with an operating system or ROM-based program.
8) The interrupt enable flag is used to allow or disallow interrupts. The STI and CLI instructions are used to manipulate the interrupt enable flag.
9) The external interrupt will be processed normally unless interrupts are disabled.
10) ESC.
11) The LOCK instruction is provided for multiple CPUs sharing the same memory bus. It allows one CPU to have complete control of the bus for the duration of an instruction execution.
12) The table will be:

```
HEXTAB DB  '01235456789ABCDEF'
```

We can convert a hexadecimal digit with the following:

```
MOV   BX, OFFSET HEXTAB
XLAT  HEXTAB
```

The 80186/80188 Extensions

The 80186 and 80188 microprocessors are improved versions of the 8086 and 8088. They include a number of new hardware features and ten new instructions. As an added plus, the 80186/80188 is between 30 and 50 percent faster than the 8086/8088. The relationship between the 80188 and the 80186 is exactly the same as between the 8088 and the 8086. The 80188 has an 8-bit data bus; the 80186 has a 16-bit data bus. From a programming perspective, they are identical. All the instructions of the 8086/8088 are also found on the 80186/80188. The object code or machine language is identical.

Most of the additional hardware features will not be of interest to the beginning assembly language programmer. In fact, several of the new hardware features will be of interest only to the computer designer. The new hardware features are:

1. Ten new instructions.
2. A chip select logic unit.
3. Two independent high-speed DMA channels.
4. Three programmable timers.
5. A programmable interrupt controller.
6. A clock generator.

To the programmer, the new hardware features look like peripheral devices. No new hardware instructions are needed to program these devices. Since the details concerning these hardware features tend to be complex and dependent on each particular computer, I will not attempt to cover the details. You should consult Intel publication number 210911-001, *iAPX 86/88, 186/188 User's Manual—Programmer's Reference,* for the specifics.

In this chapter we will concentrate on the totally new 80186/80188 instructions, and their enhancements to some existing instructions.

Input/Output

Two new input/output instructions are included, INS and OUTS. These input/output instructions operate like the string instructions. The general format of the input string instruction is:

INS   destination,port

The destination is an address contained in the DI register. The port number must be specified in the DX register. An immediate value cannot be used as it was with the IN and OUT instructions. The repeat prefix REP is used with this instruction. The CX register must be set up with the count of the number of bytes or words to be transferred. The following instructions will input 128 bytes from port number 1F00H:

```
MOV      CX,128
MOV      AX,DS
MOV      ES,AX
MOV      DI,OFFSET BUFFER
CLD
MOV      DX,01F00H
REP INS  BUFFER,DX
          .
          .
          .
;DATA SEGMENT
          .
BUFFER  DB      128 DUP(?)
          .
          .
```

Remember that we must set up the DI register to point to the string, which is located in the extra segment. In this case, ES is set to DS so that the string can be placed in the data segment. The CLD instruction makes sure that the DI register is incremented after each byte is stored.

The OUTS instruction works exactly like the INS instruction, except that the direction of the data transfer is reversed. The SI register is used to hold the address of the source string. The following instructions transfer 1000 words to port 20H:

```
MOV CX,1000
MOV SI,OFFSET BUFFER
CLD
MOV DX,020H
REP OUTS DX,BUFFER
          .
          .
;DATA SEGMENT
          .
BUFFER  DW      1000 DUP(?)
          .
          .
```

SELF-CHECK

1) What is the difference between the 80186 and the 80188?
2) How much faster is the 80186/80188 than the 8086/8088?
3) Does the 80186/80188 include any new instructions that are needed for the other new hardware features?
4) What are the new hardware features of the 80186/80188?
5) What repeat prefix is used with the INS and OUTS instructions?
6) Write the instructions necessary to input 256 words from port 100H to a buffer in the extra segment at BUFF.

1) The 80186 transfers 16 bits at a time to and from memory, while the 80188 transfers only 8. This is the same relationship as between the 8086 and 8088.
2) Between 30 and 50 percent faster.
3) No, the additional hardware features are all programmed as if they were peripheral devices.
4) a) Ten new instructions.
   b) A chip select logic unit.
   c) Two independent high-speed DMA channels.
   d) Three programmable timers.
   e) A programmable interrupt controller.
   f) A clock generator.
5) REP is used while the CX register contains the count.
6)
```
MOV    CX, 256
MOV    DX, 100H
MOV    DI, OFFSET BUFF
CLD
REP INS BUFF, DX
```

Stack Instructions

Two new stack instructions are provided that allow the programmer to save and restore the eight general purpose registers. You probably recall from Chapter 7 that we used a series of PUSH instructions to save the registers, and a series of POP instructions to restore the registers. This operation is most often performed when calling a procedure. The two new instructions are:

PUSHA   Push all 8 registers
POPA   Pop all 8 registers

The order in which the registers are pushed is AX, CX, DX, BX, SP, BP, SI, and DI. Naturally, the registers must be popped in the reverse order.

Since the process of pushing the registers is changing the value of the stack pointer (SP), the question arises as to what value of SP is actually pushed onto the stack. The answer is that the value of SP used is the value of

SP just prior to the execution of the PUSHA instruction. When the POPA instruction is executed, the value of SP is popped from the stack and thrown away. If a PUSHA and POPA pair is used, the value of SP that is thrown away is the same as the value that SP assumes after the POPA instruction completes. You must be careful that a PUSHA/POPA pair is used. If you try to use POPA without the proper stack contents, the registers will be restored with whatever happens to be on the stack at the time.

If you wish to save and restore the registers when calling a procedure, you would do it like this:

```
PUSHA
CALL    MYPROC
POPA
```

As I mentioned in Chapter 8, the registers can also be saved and restored by the procedure. In that case, the first instruction of the procedure would be a PUSHA. A POPA would be executed just prior to the procedure return.

```
MYPROC  PROC    NEAR
        PUSHA
        .
        .               ;WE CAN NOW USE ALL REGISTERS
        .
        POPA
        RET
MYPROC  ENDP
```

The 80186/80188 also allows an immediate value to be pushed onto the stack. A new form of the PUSH instruction is allowed. A 16-bit, or sign extended 8-bit value, is used as the source operand. Here are some examples:

```
PUSH    0
PUSH    10
PUSH    12345
PUSH    -1
```

This instruction is especially useful when we are passing constant arguments to a procedure by using the stack.

Immediate Addressing Extensions

A number of other instructions, in addition to the PUSH instruction, have been extended to allow an immediate operand. The entire group of shifts and rotates can now be used with an immediate value to specify the number of bits to shift or rotate. These instructions are:

```
SHL/SAL     ROL
SHR         ROR
SAR         RCL
            RCR
```

The following are now legal instructions:

```
ROL    AX, 8
SHR    BYTE PTR [BX], 3
RCR    MEMVAR, 10
```

A special version of the IMUL instruction also allows an immediate value. This is the only arithmetic instruction that has been extended. The form of this instruction is:

```
IMUL    destreg,source,immediate
```

The destination register must be one of the eight general purpose registers. The source may be a register or a memory location. It is always a 16-bit operand. The immediate value can be either an 8- or a 16-bit constant. If it is 8 bits, it is sign-extended to 16 bits. Only the lower 16 bits of the result are stored in the destination register. The source and destination can be the same register.

For example, we can multiply the AX register by 10 by merely using the following instruction:

```
IMUL    AX,AX,10
```

To multiply a word variable named COUNT by 100_{16} and to store the result in the register CX, we would write:

```
IMUL    CX,COUNT,0100H
```

SELF-CHECK

1) What registers are pushed and popped with the PUSHA and POPA instructions?
2) Which of these registers is handled differently from the others, and how?
3) Write the instruction necessary to push the value 256 onto the stack.
4) What instructions besides PUSH have been extended to allow an immediate operand, but are otherwise no different?
5) Write the instruction necessary to:
   a) Shift AX arithmetically left by 3 bits.
   b) Rotate variable MASK right by 4 bits without including the carry bit.
6) Write the instruction necessary to multiply a word variable at an offset specified by the contents of BX by the constant −100. The result is to be left in the AX register.

1) AX, BX, CX, DX, BX, BP, SI, and DI.
2) When SP is popped, its value is thrown away.
3) PUSH   256
4) All shifts and rotates.

5) a) SAL   AX, 3

   b) ROR   MASK, 4

6) IMUL   AX, WORD PTR [BX], −100

High-Level Language Extensions

More and more high-level languages are being implemented and used on 8086 family-based microcomputers. In order to allow more efficient object code to be generated by the compilers for these languages, the 80186/80188 includes three new instructions. These instructions are ENTER, LEAVE, and BOUND. ENTER and LEAVE are used to manage the stack during a procedure call. BOUND is used to check an array index to make sure it is within acceptable limits. While these instructions are primarily designed to be used by a high-level language, the assembly language programmer can also use them.

In order to understand the use of the ENTER and LEAVE instructions, you must first understand the concept of a *stack frame*. When we discussed procedures in Chapter 8, you will recall that we used the stack for holding the return address. The CALL and RET instructions were used in conjunction with the stack. We also mentioned ways in which the stack could be used to pass arguments to the procedure. Many high-level languages are implemented in such a way that, in addition to using the stack for saving the return address and passing parameters, they also use the stack for variable storage. The variables that are stored on the stack rather than in other parts of memory are referred to as *automatic* or *local* variables. Each time a procedure is called, a new set of these automatic variables is created. When the procedure returns to its caller, these automatic variables are destroyed.

Each time a procedure is called, the stack pointer is advanced by an amount large enough to accommodate the return address, the procedure arguments, and the automatic variables. The space on the stack occupied by this information for one procedure is a stack frame. As each procedure is called, a new stack frame is created. As each procedure returns to its caller, the stack frame is released. The number of stack frames present at any one time is equal to the depth or level of the procedure calls. If procedure A calls B, which in turn calls C, then we would have three stack frames. Figure 13 shows such a situation. By convention, register BP is used to hold a pointer to the current stack frame. SP always points to the last location on the stack to which a value has been pushed.

As a procedure gains control, it can access its arguments as positive offsets from the current frame pointer held in BP. If the return address is for a near procedure, it will be one word in length. Therefore, the arguments on the stack are at BP+4, BP+6, etc. At each procedure entry, the previous frame pointer (in BP) is pushed onto the stack before BP is set to its new

A STACK FRAME   THE STACK

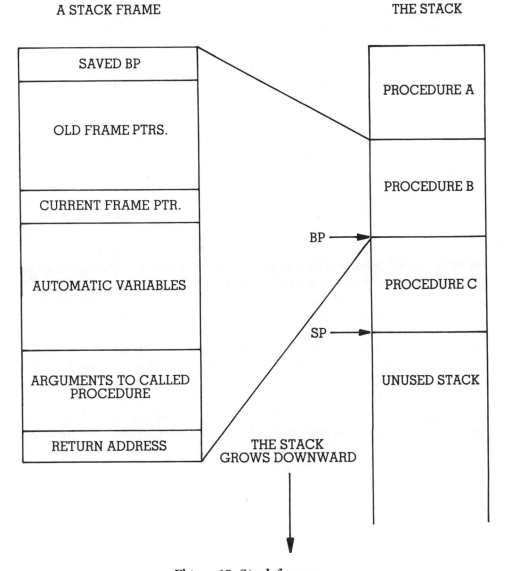

Figure 13. Stack frames.

value. Additionally, any stack space for automatic variables must be reserved. These local variables are referenced as negative offsets from the current frame pointer held in BP. Remember, the stack grows downward. The local variables would be at BP−2, BP−4, BP−6, etc. These steps would normally be done with the following instructions:

```
PUSH   BP         ;SAVE PREVIOUS FRAME PTR.
MOV    BP, SP     ;SET UP NEW FRAME POINTER
SUB    SP, n      ;RESERVE N BYTES
```

Just prior to the procedure return, the stack space for the automatic variables must be released and the frame pointer in BP reset to the caller's frame. This is accomplished with the following instructions:

```
MOV    SP, BP   ;CLEAN UP STACK
POP    BP       ;RESTORE PREVIOUS FRAME POINTER
```

The ENTER and LEAVE instructions perform the above steps automatically. We would place an ENTER instruction at the beginning of each procedure and a LEAVE instruction just before the procedure's RET instruction. The general form of the ENTER instruction is:

```
ENTER   auto,level
```

The auto operand specifies the number of bytes to reserve for automatic variables. This is the value subtracted from the stack pointer. Level is an additional operand that allows previous and current frame pointers to be copied onto the current stack. Figure 13 shows these frame pointers as optional. If the level specified is zero, then no frame pointers are pushed onto the stack. If level 1 is specified, then only the current frame pointer is pushed. For each level above 1, a previous frame pointer is obtained from the previous frames list. If the level is incremented for each nested procedure call, the current frame will always have a complete list of *all* the previous frame pointers. This allows a high-level language to access the automatic variables at all previous procedure levels. The exact use of this mechanism is really beyond the scope of this book. However, assembly language programmers may find ENTER and LEAVE at level zero to be useful. For this case, the action of ENTER is exactly as above. LEAVE is equivalent to the above instructions, regardless of the level used with ENTER. The following instructions illustrate the use of ENTER and LEAVE:

```
MYPROC   PROC   NEAR
         ENTER  n, 0
           .
           .
           .
         LEAVE
         RET
MYPROC   ENDP
```

The final instruction that is new on the 80186/80188 is the BOUND instruction. This instruction is used to check that an array index is within prescribed limits. The array index must be a 16-bit value, and it is placed in one of the general purpose registers, for example, BX. The upper and lower bounds are placed in two consecutive words in memory. If the index is less than the first word in memory or greater than the second word in memory, an interrupt type 5 is generated. You must set up the type 5 interrupt vector as we did in Chapter 13. The following instructions illustrate how we would test an array index to determine whether or not it is between 1 and 100. If it is not, control passes to label OUTB.

```
        MOV     AX,0
        MOV     ES,AX   ;SET TO BASE OF INTERRUPT
                        ;VECTORS
        MOV     BX,4*5  ;TYPE 5 INTERRUPT
        MOV     AX,OFFSET OUTB
        MOV     ES:WORD PTR [BX],AX     ;SET BASE
                                        ;AND OFFSET
        MOV     ES:WORD PTR [BX]+2,CS  ;OF OUTB
        MOV     BX,ARRAYINDEX
        BOUND   BX,BOUNDS  ;CHECK BOUNDS
            .              ;HERE IF OK
            .
OUTB:       .              ;HERE IF OUT OF BOUNDS
            .
            .
;DATA SEGMENT
BOUNDS  WORD    1, 100 ;ARRAY BOUNDS
```

What you do when control passes to OUTB is up to you. However, you must remember that an interrupt has been generated and that the return address and flags have been pushed onto the stack. In addition, interrupts have been disabled. Unless you execute an IRET instruction, you should enable external interrupts with an STI instruction and clean up the stack. If you add 6 to SP, the stack pointer will be at its value before the BOUND instruction is executed. If the interrupt handler is the same for all bounds tests, you only have to initialize the vector once, not before each BOUND is executed.

SELF-TEST
1) Can you run 8086/8088 programs on the 80186/80188?
2) What is the destination of an INS instruction?
3) What is the source of an OUTS instruction?
4) Can we use an immediate value for the port number with the INS and OUTS instructions?
5) In what order does the PUSHA instruction push the registers?
6) Using only PUSH and POP, clear the AX register.
7) What new instructions are provided for the support of high-level languages?
8) What is a stack frame?
9) Where are automatic or local variables placed?
10) Which register is used to hold a pointer to the current stack frame?
11) Write the instructions necessary to set up a procedure named COMPUTE that requires 20 bytes of automatic storage.
12) Write the instructions necessary to check whether an array bound in register DX is within the range −1000 to +1000. If not, control should pass to label BNDERR.

1) Yes, but not necessarily vice versa if the new instructions or hardware features are used.
2) The offset in the extra segment specified by the contents of register DI.
3) The offset in the data segment specified by the contents of register SI.
4) No, the port number must be in register DX.
5) AX, CX, DX, BX, SP, BP, SI, and DI.
6) PUSH   0
   POP   AX
7) ENTER, LEAVE, and BOUND.
8) An area of the stack used by a procedure that is called within a high-level language. The stack frame includes the automatic variables, procedure, arguments, etc.
9) Automatic variables are placed in the stack frame of the procedure using them.
10) Register BP.

11)
```
COMPUTE    PROC    NEAR
           ENTER   20, 0
           .
           .
           .
           LEAVE
           RET
COMPUTE    ENDP
```

12)
```
           MOV     AX,0
           MOV     ES,AX    ;SET TO BASE OF
                            ;INTERRUPT VECTORS
           MOV     BX,4*5   ;TYPE 5 INTERRUPT
           MOV     AX,OFFSET BNDERR
           MOV     ES:WORD PTR [BX],AX ;SET BASE
                                       ;AND OFFSET
           MOV     ES:WORD PTR [BX]+2,CS ;OF
                                         ;BNDERR
           BOUND   DX,BOUNDS  ;CHECK BOUNDS
                   .          ;HERE IF OK
                   .
BNDERR:            .          ;HERE IF OUT OF BOUNDS
                   .
                   .
;DATA SEGMENT
BOUNDS   WORD    -1000, 100
```

CHAPTER 15

Introduction to the 80286

The 80286 is the most powerful CPU chip in the 8086 family. It can execute instructions up to six times as fast as the 8086. It includes all of the extended instructions found on the 80186/80188 and a host of new features. Among these new features are:

- Memory management.
- Task management.
- Protection mechanisms.
- Support for operating systems.

With these new features, plus its speed, the 80286 rivals or exceeds many minicomputers. The belief that this member of the 8086 family will be a dominant force in the marketplace is exemplified by the fact that IBM's latest and most sophisticated personal computer, the PC/AT, uses the 80286. As more and more companies introduce products based on the 80286, more and more software will be developed to take advantage of this chip's new features. The software most affected and aided by the new features is that of operating systems. An assembly language programmer normally will not need to use these advanced features, and normally would not be permitted to use them. However, it is always helpful to know what is going on behind the scenes.

The 80286 can operate in two modes:

1. Real address mode.
2. Protected virtual address mode (protected mode).

When operated in real address mode, the 80286 looks just like a high-performance 80186. Programs and operating systems written for the 8086, 8088, 80186, or the 80188 will run without modification. In protected mode, the 80286 shows its real power. Even so, most programs written for the other family members will run with little or no modification in protected mode.

To cover fully how to write programs using the advanced features of the 80286 would require another volume at least this size. Readers who wish to learn more details of these advanced features can find them in the following Intel publications:

1. *Introduction to the iAPX 286.*
2. *iAPX 286 Hardware Reference Manual.*
3. *iAPX 286 Programmer's Reference Manual.*
4. *iAPX 286 Operating Systems Writer's Guide.*

For the remainder of this chapter, I will briefly describe each of the advanced features.

SELF-CHECK

1) Besides increased speed, what are the new features of the 80286?
2) What type of software will take best advantage of the extended features of the 80286?
3) What are the two operating modes of the 80286?
4) In what mode does the 80286 look like a fast 80186?

---

1) Memory management, task management, protection mechanisms, and support for operating systems.
2) Operating systems.
3) Real address mode, and protected virtual address mode.
4) Real address mode.

Memory Management

All other members of the 8086 family are restricted to 2^{16} bytes or 1 megabyte of physical memory. Each of the four segment registers can be used to reference up to 64K of this 1 megabyte of physical memory. The 80286 allows 16 times as much physical memory, or 2^{24} bytes. Unfortunately, we are still restricted because each segment register can reference only 64K bytes at a time. Nevertheless, having 16 megabytes of physical memory can be very useful.

The real advantage provided by the 80286 is that in protected mode the contents of a segment register no longer represent a paragraph address in physical memory. Instead, the contents of a segment register is a *segment selector*. This segment selector is, in turn, mapped to an appropriate area of physical memory. Of the 16 bits of a segment register, 14 are used as the segment selector, allowing 2^{14} or 16,384 possible 64K segments. A little arithmetic shows that $2^{14} \times 2^{16} = 2^{30}$, or 1 gigabyte, of addressing is possible.

How can we have a 1-gigabyte address space with a maximum of only 16 megabytes of physical memory? The answer is that a maximum of only 16 megabytes of this addressing space can be in physical memory at one time. Just as we may not have 1 entire megabyte of physical memory for an 8086, we may not have a full 16 megabytes on an 80286. On the 8086, we are always forced to set a segment register to a paragraph address that corresponds to an area of physical memory that actually exists. This is not so on the 80286.

A reference to an address consisting of a segment selector and offset is actually a *virtual address*. It may or may not exist in physical memory at the time it is referenced. Unlike the 8086, the 80286 allows memory references to these virtual addresses. If a reference is made to an address not currently mapped to physical memory, control is passed to the operating system. The operating system can then bring a segment into memory when it is needed and return control to the program. Segments that are not in physical memory are kept on a secondary storage device, such as a disk. The techniques used by the operating system are for *virtual memory management*. A good operating systems text can provide you with information about how to design an operating system for a virtual memory. The important point here is that the 80286 provides memory management hardware right on the chip. Without these hardware features, it is not possible to implement a virtual memory, no matter how clever the operating system is.

Let's take a closer look at how a value in a segment selector is mapped to physical memory. As I mentioned earlier, 14 bits of the segment selector are used to specify the segment. Of the 2^{14} possible values, half are mapped the same for all users (tasks); the other half are mapped on an individual user basis. The mapping is performed by information stored in a descriptor table. The global descriptor table (GDT) provides the mapping for the 2^{13} segments that all tasks share. A local descriptor table (LDT) is provided for each task in the system.

Each entry in the GDT or LDT contains the actual physical address and size of the segment. The segment selector's value is used as the index into the GDT or LDT. The GDT and LDT entries also provide protection information, which will be discussed below. Since not all of the 2^{14} segments can be in memory at the same time, the descriptor table entry contains a bit which indicates whether the segment is present. If it is not present, then the operating system must allocate physical memory space, transfer the segment data from secondary storage, and finally set up the descriptor entry. All this can take place transparently in the program's execution. Figure 14 on the following page shows how the GDT and the LDT are used for mapping.

SELF-CHECK

1) How much physical memory can the 80286 have?
2) In protected mode, how large is the address space?
3) What happens if reference is made to a virtual address that is not in physical memory?
4) How many values may a segment selector have?
5) How are these segment selector values divided up?

---

1) 16 megabytes.
2) 1 gigabyte.
3) Control is passed to the operating system so that it can bring in the segment from a secondary storage device, such as a disk.

4) 16,384 or 2^{14}.
5) Half are mapped for all users by the GDT; the other half are mapped on a per-user basis by the LDT.

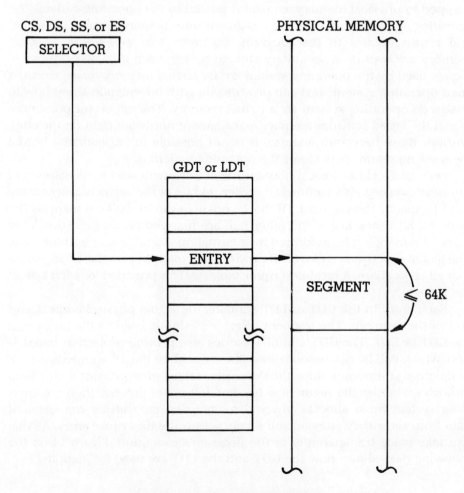

Figure 14. GDT and LDT usage.

Protection Mechanisms

The 80286 is designed to support multitasking operating systems. In order to be able to build a reliable multitasking operating system, the CPU must include protection mechanisms. Although not found on most microprocessors that support single users, protection mechanisms are useful for all operating systems. The term *multitasking* refers to the ability of a system to support the execution of several jobs at once. These jobs may be interactive users or the individual jobs of a batch processing system.

Basically, two types of protection are needed for a multitasking system:

- Protection of the operating system from any task.
- Protection of one task from another task.

The 80286 provides both of these mechanisms by restricting access to parts of the virtual address space. Every segment has an associated privilege level. There are four privilege levels. Segments can be further protected by marking them as code or as data and by indicating whether they can be written or just read.

The operating system is protected from tasks primarily by the four levels of privilege. Figure 15 shows how this works. The most sensitive part of the operating system, the *kernel*, is assigned privilege level 0. Other parts of the

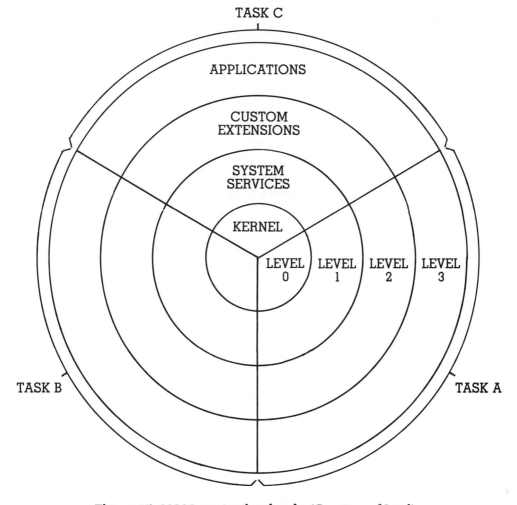

Figure 15. 80286 protection levels. (Courtesy of Intel)

operating system are assigned levels 1 and 2. The application program runs in level 3. Access to an inner level from an outer level is restricted. The innermost level, level 0, is the most privileged level. If a task executing at one privilege level wishes to call a procedure at an inner privilege level, a special call is made. Rather than call the procedure segment directly, a call is made to a special *call gate*. This call gate mediates the change in privilege level.

Tasks are protected from each other primarily by management of the virtual address space. When the operating system transfers control to a task, its virtual address space is set up so that only its own segments and those of the operating system are addressable. Any segments that are shared between tasks can appear in the address space of each task. By making these segments *read only*, they can be protected from modification.

Task Management

One of the main responsibilities of the operating system in a multitasking environment is to control the switching from one task to another. This *context switch* involves saving the state of the interrupted task and restoring the state of the next task to be run. The complex operation can be performed in 22 microseconds by a single instruction on the 80286.

Associated with each task is a *Task State Segment* (TSS). This special segment contains the current state of a task, including the registers, flags, and address space. When the operating system initiates a context switch, the state of the currently running task is saved in its TSS, and the state of the new task is restored from the new task's TSS.

SELF-TEST

1) How much faster is the 80286 than the 8086?
2) Under what conditions will 8086, 8088, 80186, and 80188 programs run on the 80286 without modification?
3) What are the two descriptor tables?
4) How does the 80286 know whether a reference is being made to a segment that is not in physical memory?
5) What is multitasking?
6) Why is protection needed for a multitasking system?
7) How many privilege levels are there?
8) Other than the privilege levels, what other protection is available with the 80286?
9) What is a call gate?
10) What is a context switch?

===

1) Approximately 6 times as fast.
2) If the 80286 is used in real address mode.

3) The global descriptor table (GDT) and the local descriptor table (LDT).

4) A special bit in the descriptor table entry indicates whether or not a segment is present in physical memory.

5) The concurrent execution of more than one program. Each program can be from a different user, or a single user may be running several different programs.

6) So that programs with errors or malicious users do not corrupt either the operating system or other users.

7) 4

8) We can mark a segment as code or as data and limit the ability to read or write the segment.

9) A call gate mediates the change in privilege level when one procedure calls another.

10) A context switch is the passing of control from one task to another.

ASCII Character Codes

Decimal	Octal	Hex	ASCII	Decimal	Octal	Hex	ASCII
0	000	00	NUL	32	040	20	SP
1	001	01	SOH	33	041	21	!
2	002	02	STX	34	042	22	"
3	003	03	ETX	35	043	23	#
4	004	04	EOT	36	044	24	$
5	005	05	ENQ	37	045	25	%
6	006	06	ACK	38	046	26	&
7	007	07	BEL	39	047	27	'
8	010	08	BS	40	050	28	(
9	011	09	HT	41	051	29	)
10	012	0A	LF	42	052	2A	*
11	013	0B	VT	43	053	2B	+
12	014	0C	FF	44	054	2C	,
13	015	0D	CR	45	055	2D	-
14	016	0E	SO	46	056	2E	.
15	017	0F	SI	47	057	2F	/
16	020	10	DLE	48	060	30	0
17	021	11	DC1	49	061	31	1
18	022	12	DC2	50	062	32	2
19	023	13	DC3	51	063	33	3
20	024	14	DC4	52	064	34	4
21	025	15	NAK	53	065	35	5
22	026	16	SYN	54	066	36	6
23	027	17	ETB	55	067	37	7
24	030	18	CAN	56	070	38	8
25	031	19	EM	57	071	39	9
26	032	1A	SUB	58	072	3A	:
27	033	1B	ESC	59	073	3B	;
28	034	1C	FS	60	074	3C	<
29	035	1D	GS	61	075	3D	=
30	036	1E	RS	62	076	3E	>
31	037	1F	US	63	077	3F	?

Decimal	Octal	Hex	ASCII	Decimal	Octal	Hex	ASCII
64	100	40	@	96	140	60	`
65	101	41	A	97	141	61	a
66	102	42	B	98	142	62	b
67	103	43	C	99	143	63	c
68	104	44	D	100	144	64	d
69	105	45	E	101	145	65	e
70	106	46	F	102	146	66	f
71	107	47	G	103	147	67	g
72	110	48	H	104	150	68	h
73	111	49	I	105	151	69	i
74	112	4A	J	106	152	6A	j
75	113	4B	K	107	153	6B	k
76	114	4C	L	108	154	6C	l
77	115	4D	M	109	155	6D	m
78	116	4E	N	110	156	6E	n
79	117	4F	O	111	157	6F	o
80	120	50	P	112	160	70	p
81	121	51	Q	113	161	71	q
82	122	52	R	114	162	72	r
83	123	53	S	115	163	73	s
84	124	54	T	116	164	74	t
85	125	55	U	117	165	75	u
86	126	56	V	118	166	76	v
87	127	57	W	119	167	77	w
88	130	58	X	120	170	78	x
89	131	59	Y	121	171	79	y
90	132	5A	Z	122	172	7A	z
91	133	5B	[	123	173	7B	{
92	134	5C		124	174	7C		
93	135	5D	]	125	175	7D	}
94	136	5E	^	126	176	7E	~
95	137	5F	—	127	177	7F	DEL

Standard I/O Procedures

```
;STANDARD I/O PROCEDURES FOR THE MICROSOFT ASSEMBLER
;
BDOS     EQU    21H          ;OS INTERRUPT NO.
CR       EQU    0DH
LF       EQU    0AH
;
;
INDEC    PROC   NEAR
         PUSH   BX           ;SAVE REGISTERS
         PUSH   CX
         PUSH   DX
         XOR    BX,BX        ;CLEAR N
INDEC0:  PUSH   BX           ;SAVE N
         CALL   GETC         ;GET NEXT CHARACTER
         POP    BX           ;RESTORE N
         CMP    AL,'0'       ;< 0?
         JB     INDEC2       ;YES
         CMP    AL,'9'       ;> 9?
         JA     INDEC2       ;YES
         SUB    AL,'0'       ;GET DECIMAL DIGIT
INDEC1:  PUSH   AX           ;SAVE DIGIT
         MOV    AX,10        ;MULTIPLY N BY 10
         MUL    BX
         MOV    BX,AX
         POP    AX           ;RESTORE DIGIT
         XOR    AH,AH
         ADD    BX,AX        ;ADD IN DIGIT
         JMP    INDEC0       ;GET NEXT DIGIT
INDEC2:  MOV    AX,BX        ;RETURN N IN AX
         POP    DX           ;RESTORE REGISTERS
         POP    CX
         POP    BX
         RET                 ;RETURN TO CALLER
INDEC    ENDP
;
OUTDEC   PROC   NEAR
         PUSH   AX           ;SAVE REGISTERS
         PUSH   BX
         PUSH   CX
         PUSH   DX
         XOR    CL,CL        ;INITIALIZE DIGIT COUNT
         MOV    BX,10        ;SET UP DIVISOR
OUTD1:   XOR    DX,DX        ;ZERO HIGH ORDER WORD OF DIVIDEND
         DIV    BX           ;DIVIDE BY 10
```

```
                PUSH    DX          ;SAVE REMAINDER ON STACK
                INC     CL          ;BUMP COUNT
                CMP     AX,0        ;ANYTHING LEFT?
                JA      OUTD1       ;YES, GET NEXT DIGIT
                XOR     CH,CH       ;ZERO HIGH ORDER BYTE OF COUNT FOR LOOP
        OUTD2:  POP     AX          ;GET A DIGIT FROM STACK
                ADD     AL,'0'      ;GET CHARACTER CODE FROM DIGIT
                PUSH    CX          ;SAVE CX
                CALL    PUTC        ;OUTPUT THE DIGIT
                POP     CX          ;GET CX BACK
                LOOP    OUTD2       ;LOOP TIL CL=0
                POP     DX          ;RESTORE REGISTERS
                POP     CX
                POP     BX
                POP     AX
                RET                 ;RETURN TO CALLER
        OUTDEC  ENDP
        ;
        NEWLINE PROC    NEAR
                PUSH    AX          ;SAVE REGISTERS
                PUSH    BX
                PUSH    CX
                PUSH    DX
                MOV     AL,CR       ;GET CAR RET CHARACTER
                CALL    PUTC        ;OUTPUT
                MOV     AL,LF       ;GET LINE FEED CHARACTER
                CALL    PUTC        ;OUTPUT
                POP     DX          ;RESTORE REGISTERS
                POP     CX
                POP     BX
                POP     AX
                RET                 ;RETURN TO CALLER
        NEWLINE ENDP
        ;
        PUTC    PROC    NEAR
                PUSH    AX          ;SAVE REGISTERS
                PUSH    BX
                PUSH    CX
                PUSH    DX
                MOV     DL,AL
                MOV     AH,02H      ;CALL OS FUNCTION 2
                INT     BDOS
                POP     DX          ;RESTORE REGISTERS
                POP     CX
                POP     BX
                POP     AX
                RET                 ;RETURN TO CALLER
        PUTC    ENDP
        ;
        GETC    PROC    NEAR
                PUSH    BX          ;SAVE REGISTERS
                PUSH    CX
                PUSH    DX
                MOV     AH,01H      ;CALL OS FUNCTION 1
                INT     BDOS
                POP     DX          ;RESTORE REGISTERS
                POP     CX
                POP     BX
                RET
        GETC    ENDP
```

```
;STANDARD I/O PROCEDURES FOR THE DIGITAL RESEARCH
;ASM86 ASSEMBLER
;
BDOS     EQU    224           ;OS INTERRUPT NO.
CR       EQU    0DH
LF       EQU    0AH
;
INDEC:   PUSH   BX            ;SAVE REGISTERS
         PUSH   CX
         PUSH   DX
         XOR    BX,BX         ;CLEAR N
INDEC0:  PUSH   BX            ;SAVE N
         CALL   GETC          ;GET NEXT CHARACTER
         POP    BX            ;RESTORE N
         CMP    AL,'0'        ;< 0?
         JB     INDEC2        ;YES
         CMP    AL,'9'        ;> 9?
         JA     INDEC2        ;YES
         SUB    AL,'0'        ;GET DECIMAL DIGIT
INDEC1:  PUSH   AX            ;SAVE DIGIT
         MOV    AX,10         ;MULTIPLY N BY 10
         MUL    BX
         MOV    BX,AX
         POP    AX            ;RESTORE DIGIT
         XOR    AH,AH
         ADD    BX,AX         ;ADD IN DIGIT
         JMP    INDEC0        ;GET NEXT DIGIT
INDEC2:  MOV    AX,BX         ;RETURN N IN AX
         POP    DX            ;RESTORE REGISTERS
         POP    CX
         POP    BX
         RET                  ;RETURN TO CALLER
;
OUTDEC:  PUSH   AX            ;SAVE REGISTERS
         PUSH   BX            ;       "
         PUSH   CX            ;       "
         PUSH   DX            ;       "
         XOR    CL,CL         ;INITIALIZE DIGIT COUNT
         MOV    BX,10         ;SET UP DIVISOR
OUTD1:   XOR    DX,DX         ;ZERO HIGH ORDER WORD OF DIVIDEND
         DIV    BX            ;DIVIDE BY 10
         PUSH   DX            ;SAVE REMAINDER ON STACK
         INC    CL            ;BUMP COUNT
         CMP    AX,0          ;ANYTHING LEFT?
         JA     OUTD1         ;YES, GET NEXT DIGIT
         XOR    CH,CH         ;ZERO HIGH ORDER BYTE OF COUNT FOR LOOP
OUTD2:   POP    AX            ;GET A DIGIT FROM STACK
         ADD    AL,'0'        ;GET CHARACTER CODE FROM DIGIT
         PUSH   CX            ;SAVE CX
         CALL   PUTC          ;OUTPUT THE DIGIT
         POP    CX            ;GET CX BACK
         LOOP   OUTD2         ;LOOP TIL CL=0
         POP    DX            ;RESTORE REGISTERS
         POP    CX            ;       "
         POP    BX            ;       "
         POP    AX            ;       "
         RET                  ;RETURN TO CALLER
;
NEWLINE: PUSH   AX            ;SAVE REGISTERS
         PUSH   BX
         PUSH   CX
         PUSH   DX
         MOV    AL,CR         ;GET CAR RET CHARACTER
         CALL   PUTC          ;OUTPUT
         MOV    AL,LF         ;GET LINE FEED CHARACTER
```

```
            CALL    PUTC        ;OUTPUT
            POP     DX          ;RESTORE REGISTERS
            POP     CX
            POP     BX
            POP     AX
            RET                 ;RETURN TO CALLER
;
PUTC:       PUSH    AX          ;SAVE REGISTERS
            PUSH    BX
            PUSH    CX
            PUSH    DX
MOV         DL,AL
            MOV     CL,02H      ;CALL OS FUNCTION 2
            INT     BDOS
            POP     DX          ;RESTORE REGISTERS
            POP     CX
            POP     BX
            POP     AX
            RET                 ;RETURN TO CALLER
;
GETC:       PUSH    BX          ;SAVE REGISTERS
            PUSH    CX
            PUSH    DX
            MOV     CL,01H      ;CALL OS FUNCTION 1
            INT     BDOS
            POP     DX          ;RESTORE REGISTERS
            POP     CX
            POP     BX
            RET
```

APPENDIX C

Program Shells

```
;PROGRAM SHELL FOR THE DIGITAL RESEARCH ASSEMBLER
;USES CP/M
;
        TITLE        'CP/M SHELL'
;
        CSEG
;
        .
        .
        .
        <CODE SEGMENT GOES HERE>
        .
        .
        RETF          ;RETURN TO CP/M86
        .
        .
        <STANDARD I/O PROCEDURES GO HERE>
        .
        .
        .
;
        DSEG
        ORG          100H
;
        .
        .
        .
        <DATA SEGMENT GOES HERE>
        .
        .
; NOTE — AT LEAST ONE BYTE OF DATA MUST BE PRESENT
;           FOR CP/M-86 TO LOAD CORRECTLY
        END
;PROGRAM SHELL FOR USE WITH THE MICROSOFT (IBM) ASSEMBLER
;USES MS-DOS (PC-DOS)
;
                TITLE   MICROSOFT SHELL
;
DSEG    SEGMENT PUBLIC 'DATA'
;
        .
        .
```

```
                <DATA SEGMENT GOES HERE>
                .
                .
;
DSEG    ENDS
;
SSEG    SEGMENT STACK 'STACK'
        DB      64 DUP ('STACK   ')
SSEG    ENDS
;
CSEG    SEGMENT PUBLIC 'CODE'
;
        ASSUME CS:CSEG,DS:DSEG,SS:SSEG
;
START   PROC    FAR             ;SET UP RETURN
        PUSH    DS
        XOR     AX,AX
        PUSH    AX
        MOV     AX,DSEG         ;INIT DS
        MOV     DS,AX
;
                .
                .
                <CODE SEGMENT GOES HERE>
                .
                .
;
        RET                     ;RETURN TO OS
START   ENDP
                .
                .
                <STANDARD I/O PROCEDURES GO HERE>
                .
                .
;
CSEG    ENDS
;
        END     START
```

Instruction Reference

Key to following Instruction Set Reference Pages

IDENTIFIER	USED IN	EXPLANATION
destination	data transfer, bit manipulation	A register or memory location that may contain data operated on by the instruction, and which receives (is replaced by) the result of the operation.
source	data transfer, arithmetic, bit manipulation	A register, memory location or immediate value that is used in the operation, but is not altered by the instruction.
source-table	XLAT	Name of memory translation table addressed by register BX.
target	JMP, CALL	A label to which control is to be transferred directly, or a register or memory location whose *content* is the address of the location to which control is to be transferred indirectly.
short-label	cond. transfer, iteration control	A label to which control is to be conditionally transferred; must lie within −128 to +127 bytes of the first byte of the next instruction.
accumulator	IN, OUT	Register AX for word transfers, AL for bytes.
port	IN, OUT	An I/O port number; specified as an immediate value of 0-255, or register DX (which contains port number in range 0-64k).
source-string	string ops.	Name of a string in memory that is addressed by register SI; used only to identify string as byte or word and specify segment override, if any. This string is used in the operation, but is not altered.
dest-string	string ops.	Name of string in memory that is addressed by register DI; used only to identify string as byte or word. This string receives (is replaced by) the result of the operation.
count	shifts, rotates	Specifies number of bits to shift or rotate; written as immediate value 1 or register CL (which contains the count in the range 0-255).
interrupt-type	INT	Immediate value of 0-255 identifying interrupt pointer number.
optional-pop-value	RET	Number of bytes (0-64k, ordinarily an even number) to discard from stack.
external-opcode	ESC	Immediate value (0-63) that is encoded in the instruction for use by an external processor.
above-below	conditional jumps	Above and below refer to the relationship of two unsigned values.
greater-less	conditional jumps	Greater and less refer to the relationship of two signed values.

Reprinted with permission of Intel Corporation. No part of this publication may be reproduced in any form or by any means without prior written consent of Intel Corporation. Intel Corporation assumes no responsibility for any errors that may appear in this document, nor for any error introduced in its reproduction.

Key to Operand Types

IDENTIFIER	EXPLANATION
(no operands)	No operands are written
register	An 8- or 16-bit general register
reg 16	An 16-bit general register
seg-reg	A segment register
accumulator	Register AX or AL
immediate	A constant in the range 0-FFFFH
immed8	A constant in the range 0-FFH
memory	An 8- or 16-bit memory location[1]
mem8	An 8-bit memory location[1]
mem16	A 16-bit memory location[1]
source-table	Name of 256-byte translate table
source-string	Name of string addressed by register SI
dest-string	Name of string. addressed by register DI
DX	Register DX
short-label	A label within −128 to +127 bytes of the end of the instruction
near-label	A label in current code segment
far-label	A label in another code segment
near-proc	A procedure in current code segment
far-proc	A procedure in another code segment
memptr16	A word containing the offset of the location in the current code segment to which control is to be transferred[1]
memptr32	A doubleword containing the offset and the segment base address of the location in another code segment to which control is to be transferred[1]
regptr16	A 16-bit general register containing the offset of the location in the current code segment to which control is to be transferred
repeat	A string instruction repeat prefix

[1] Any addressing mode — direct, register indirect, based, indexed, or based indexed — may be used (see Section 3.6).

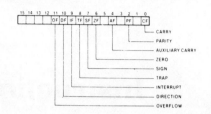

Effective Address Calculation Time (8086,88 ONLY)

EA COMPONENTS		CLOCKS*
Displacement Only		6
Base or Index Only (BX,BP,SI,DI)		5
Displacement + Base or Index (BX,BP,SI,DI)		9
Base + Index	BP + DI, BX + SI	7
	BP + SI, BX + DI	8
Displacement + Base + Index	BP + DI + DISP BX + SI + DISP	11
	BP + SI + DISP BX + DI + DISP	12

* Add 2 clocks for segment override

Notation Key

+	Addition
−	Subtraction
*	Multiplication
/	Division
%	Modulo
:	Concatenation
&	And
←	Assignment

* Not available on the 8086/8088.

AAA   ASCII ADJUST FOR ADDITION   AAA

Operation:

if ((AL) & OFH) >9 or (AF) = 1 then
    (AL) ← (AL) + 6
    (AH) ← (AH) + 1
    (AF) ← 1
(CF) ← (AF)
(AL) ← (AL) & OFH

Flags Affected:

AF, CF.
OF, PF, XF, ZF undefined

AAA Operands	Clocks	Transfers	Bytes	AAA Coding Example
(no operands)	8(8)	-	1	AAA

AAD   ASCII ADJUST FOR DIVISION   AAD

Operation:

(AL) ← (AH) * OAH + (AL)
(AH) ← 0

Flags Affected:

PF, SF, ZF.
AF, CF, OF undefined

AAD Operands	Clocks	Transfers	Bytes	AAD Coding Example
(no operands)	60(15)	-	2	AAD

AAM   ASCII ADJUST FOR MULTIPLY   AAM

Operation:

(AH) ← (AL) / OAH
(AL) ← (AL) % OAH

Flags Affected:

PF, SF, ZF.
AF, CF, OF undefined

AAM Operands	Clocks	Transfers	Bytes	AAM Coding Example
(no operands)	83(19)	-	2	AAM

AAS

ASCII ADJUST FOR SUBTRACTION

AAS

Operation:

if ((AL) & 0FH) >9 or (AF) = 1 then
  (AL) ← (AL) - 6
  (AH) ← (AH) - 1
  (AF) ← 1
(CF) ← (AF)
(AL) ← (AL) & 0FH

Flags Affected:

AF, CF.
OF, PF, SF, ZF undefined

AAS Operands	Clocks	Transfers	Bytes	AAS Coding Example
(no operands)	8(7)	-	1	AAS

ADC

ADD WITH CARRY

ADC

Operation:

if (CF) = 1 then (DEST) ← (LSRC)
  + (RSRC) + 1
else (DEST) ← (LSRC) + (RSRC)

Flags Affected:

AF, CF, OF, PF, SF, ZF

ADC Operands	Clocks	Transfers	Bytes	ADC Coding Example
register, register	3(3)	-	2	ADC AX, SI
register, memory	9(10)+EA	1	2-4	ADD DX, BETA [SI]
memory, register	16(10)+EA	2	2-4	ADC ALPHA [BX][SI],DI
register, immediate	4(4)	-	3-4	ADC BX, 256
memory, immediate	17(16)+EA	2	3-6	ADC GAMMA, 30H
accumulator, immediate	4(3-4)	-	2-3	ADC AL, 5

ADD

ADDITION

ADD

Operation:

(DEST) ← (LSRC) + (RSRC)

Flags Affected:

AF, CF, OF, PF, SF, ZF

ADD Operands	Clocks	Transfers	Bytes	ADD Coding Example
register, register	3(3)	-	2	ADD CX, DX
register, memory	9(10)+EA	1	2-4	ADD DI, [BX].ALPHA
memory, register	16(10)+EA	2	2-4	ADD TEMP, CL
register, immediate	4(4)	-	3-4	ADD CL, 2
memory, immediate	17(16)+EA	2	3-6	ADD ALPHA, 2
accumulator, immediate	4(3-4)	-	2-3	ADD AX, 200

AND   AND LOGICAL   AND

Operation:

(DEST) ← (LSRC) & (RSRC)
(CF) ← 0
(OF) ← 0

Flags Affected:

CF, OF, PF, SF, ZF.
AF undefined

AND Operands	Clocks	Transfers	Bytes	AND Coding Example
register, register	3(3)	-	2	AND AL, BL
register, memory	9(10)+EA	1	2-4	AND CX, FLAG_WORD
memory, register	16(10)+EA	2	2-4	AND ASCII [DI],AL
register, immediate	4(4)	-	3-4	AND CX, 0F0H
memory, immediate	17(16)+EA	2	3-6	AND BETA, 01H
accumulator, immediate	4(3-4)	-	2-3	AND AX, 01010000B

BOUND   DETECT VALUE OUT OF RANGE   BOUND

Operation:

If ((LSRC) < (RSRC) OR (LSRC) ≥ ((RSRC) + 2) then
    (SP) ← (SP) - 2
    ((SP) + 1 : (SP)) ←FLAGS
    (IF) ← 0
    (TF) ← 0
    (SP) ← (SP) - 2
    ((SP) + 1 : (SP)) ← (CS)
    (CS) ← (1EH)
    (SP) ← (SP) - 2
    ((SP) + 1 : (SP)) ← (IP)
    (IP) ← (1CH)

Flags Affected:

None

BOUND Operands	Clocks	Transfers	Bytes	BOUND Coding Example
register, memory*	(35)	2	2	BOUND AX, ALPHA

CALL   CALL PROCEDURE   CALL

Operation:

if Inter-Segment then
  (SP) ← (SP) - 2
  ((SP) + 1:(SP)) ← (CS)
  (CS) ← SEG
(SP) ← (SP) - 2
((SP) + 1:(SP)) ← (IP)
(IP) ← DEST

Flags Affected:

None

CALL Operands	Clocks	Transfers	Bytes	CALL Coding Examples
near-proc	19(14)	1	3	CALL NEAR_PROC
far-proc	28(23)	2	5	CALL FAR_PROC
memptr16	21(19)+EA	2	2-4	CALL PROC_TABLE [SI]
regptr16	16(13)	1	2	CALL AX
memptr32	37(38)+EA	4	2-4	CALL [BX].TASK [SI]

CBW   CONVERT BYTE TO WORD   CBW

Operation:

if (AL) < 80H then (AH) ← 0 else (AH) ← FFH

Flags Affected:

None

CBW Operands	Clocks	Transfers	Bytes	CBW Coding Example
(no operands)	2(2)	-	1	CBW

CLC   CLEAR CARRY   CLC

Operation:

(CF) ← 0

Flags Affected:

CF

CLC Operands	Clocks	Transfers	Bytes	CLC Coding Example
(no operands)	2(2)	-	1	CLC

CLD CLEAR DIRECTION FLAG CLD

Operation:

$(DF) \leftarrow 0$

Flags Affected:

DF

CLD Operands	Clocks	Transfers	Bytes	CLD Coding Example
(no operands)	2(2)	-	1	CLD

CLI CLEAR INTERRUPT-ENABLE FLAG CLI

Operation:

$(IF) \leftarrow 0$

Flags Affected:

IF

CLI Operands	Clocks	Transfers	Bytes	CLI Coding Example
(no operands)	2(2)	-	1	CLI

CMC COMPLEMENT CARRY FLAG CMC

Operation:

if (CF) = 0 then (CF) $\leftarrow$ 1 else (CF) $\leftarrow$ 0

Flags Affected:

CF

CMC Operands	Clocks	Transfers	Bytes	CMC Coding Example
(no operands)	2(2)	-	1	CMC

CMP   COMPARE   CMP

Operation:

(LSRC) - (RSRC)

Flags Affected:

AF, CF, OF, PF, SF, ZF

CMP Operands	Clocks	Transfers	Bytes	CMP Coding Examples
register, register	3(3)	-	2	CMP BX, CX
register, memory	9(10)+EA	1	2-4	CMP DH, ALPHA
memory, register	9(10)+EA	1	2-4	CMP [BP+2],SI
register, immediate	4(3)	-	3-4	CMP BL, 02H
memory, immediate	10(10)+EA	1	3-6	CMP [BX].RADAR [DI],3420H
accumulator, immediate	4(3-4)	-	2-3	CMP AL, 00010000B

CMPS   COMPARE STRING   CMPS
(BYTE OR WORD)

Operation:

(LSRC) - (RSRC)
if (DF) = 0 then
    (SI) ← (SI) + DELTA
    (DI) ← (DI) + DELTA
else
    (SI) ← (SI) - DELTA
    (DI) ← (DI) - DELTA

Flags Affected:

AF, CF, OF, PF, SF, ZF

CMPS Operands	Clocks	Transfers	Bytes	CMPS Coding Examples
dest-string, source-string	22(22)	2	1	CMPS BUFF1, BUFF2
(repeat)dest-string, source-string	9+22 (5+22/rep)	2/rep	1	REP COMPS ID, KEY

CWD   CONVERT WORD   CWD
TO DOUBLEWORD

Operation:

if (AX) < 8000H then (DX) ← 0
else (DX) ← FFFFH

Flags Affected:

None

CWD Operands	Clocks	Transfers	Bytes	CWD Coding Example
(no operands)	5(4)	-	1	CWD

DAA   DECIMAL ADJUST FOR ADDITION   DAA

Operation:

if ((AL) & 0FH) > 9 or (AF) = 1 then
  (AL) ← (AL) + 6
  (AF) ← 1
if (AL) > 9FH or (CF) = 1 then
  (AL) ← (AL) + 60H
  (CF) ← 1

Flags Affected:

AF, CF, PF, SF, ZF
OF undefined

DAA Operands	Clocks	Transfers	Bytes	DAA Coding Example
(no operands)	4(4)	-	1	DAA

DAS   DECIMAL ADJUST FOR SUBTRACTION   DAS

Operation:

if ((AL) & 0FH) >9 or (AF) = 1 then
  (AL) ← (AL) - 6
  (AF) ← 1
if (AL) > 9FH or (CF) = 1 then
  (AL) ← (AL) - 60H
  (CF) ← 1

Flags Affected:

AF, CF, PF, SF, ZF.
OF undefined

DAS Operands	Clocks	Transfers	Bytes	DAS Coding Example
(no operands)	4(4)	-	1	DAS

DEC   DECREMENT   DEC

Operation:

(DEST) ← (DEST) - 1

Flags Affected:

AF, OF, PF, SF, ZF

DEC Operands	Clocks	Transfers	Bytes	DEC Coding Example
reg16	3(3)	-	1	DEC AX
reg8	3(3)	-	2	DEC AL
memory	15(15)+EA	2	2-4	DEC ARRAY [SI]

DIV   DIVIDE   DIV

Operation:

(temp) ← (NUMR)
if (temp) / (DIVR) > MAX then the
following, in sequence
(QUO), (REM) undefined
(SP) ← (SP) - 2
((SP) + 1:(SP)) ← FLAGS
(IF) ← 0
(TF) ← 0
(SP) ← (SP) - 2
((SP) + 1:(SP)) ← (CS)
(CS) ← (2) i.e., the contents of
      memory locations 2 and 3
(SP) ← (SP) - 2
((SP) + 1:(SP)) ← (IP)
(IP) ← (0) i.e., the contents of
      locations 0 and 1
else
(QUO) ← (temp) / (DIVR), where
      / is unsigned division
(REM) ← (temp) % (DIVR) where
      % is unsigned modulo

Flags Affected:

AF, CF, OF, PF, SF, ZF undefined

DIV Operands	Clocks	Transfers	Bytes	DIV Coding Example
reg8	80-90(29)	-	2	DIV CL
reg16	144-162(38)	-	2	DIV BX
mem8	86-96			
	+EA(35)	1	2-4	DIV ALPHA
mem16	154-172			
	+EA(44)	1	2-4	DIV TABLE [SI]

ENTER   PROCEDURE ENTRY   ENTER

Operation:

Flags Affected:

None

(SP) ← (SP) - 2
((SP+1: (SP)) ← (BP)
(FP) ← (SP)
IF LEVEL > 0 then
   Repeat (Level - 1) times
      (BP) ← (BP) - 2
      (SP) ← (SP) - 2
      ((SP) +1: (SP)) ← ((BP))
   End Repeat
   (SP) ← (SP) - 2
   ((SP) +1: (SP)) ← (FP)
End if
(BP) ← (FP)
(SP) ← (SP) - (LSRC)

ENTER Operands	Clocks	Transfers	Bytes	ENTER Coding Example
Locals, level *	L=0(15) L=1(25) L>1(22+16 (n-1))	-	4	ENTER 28,3

ESC   ESCAPE   ESC

Operation:

Flags Affected:

if mod ≠ 11 then data bus ← (EA)

None

ESC Operands	Clocks	Transfers	Bytes	ESC Coding Example
immediate, memory	8(6)+EA	1	2-4	ESC 6, ARRAY [SI]
immediate, register	2(2)	-	2	ESC 20, AL

HLT   HALT   HLT

Operation: Flags Affected:

None   None

HLT Operands	Clocks	Transfers	Bytes	HLT Coding Example
(no operands)	2(2)	-	1	HLT

IDIV   INTEGER DIVIDE   IDIV

Operation: Flags Affected:

(temp) ← (NUMR)   AF, CF, OF, PF, SF, ZF undefined
if (temp) / (DIVR) > 0 and (temp)
  / (DIVR) > MAX
or (temp) / (DIVR) < 0 and (temp)
  / (DIVR) < 0 - MAX - 1 then
  (QUO), (REM) undefined
  (SP) ← (SP) - 2
  ((SP) + 1:(SP)) ← FLAGS
  (IF) ← 0
  (TF) ← 0
  (SP) ← (SP) - 2
  ((SP) + 1:(SP)) ← (CS)
  (CS) ← (2)
  (SP) ← (SP) - 2
  ((SP) + 1:(SP)) ← (IP)
  (IP) ← (0)
else
  (QUO) ← (temp) / (DIVR), where
    / is signed division
  (REM) ← (temp) % (DIVR) where
    % is signed modulo

IDIV Operands	Clocks	Transfers	Bytes	IDIV Coding Example
reg8	101-112 (44-52)	-	2	IDIV BL
reg16	165-184 (53-61)	-	2	IDIV CX
mem8	107-118 +EA(50-58)	1	2-4	IDIV DIVISOR_BYTE[SI]
mem16	171-190 +EA(59-67)	1	2-4	IDIV [BX].DIVISOR_WORD

IMUL   INTEGER MULTIPLY   IMUL

Operation:

(DEST) ← (LSRC) * (RSRC) where
   * is signed multiply
if (ext) = sign-extension of (LOW)
   then (CF) ← 0
else (CF) ← 1;
(OF) ← (CF)

Flags Affected:

CF, OF
AF, PF, SF, ZF undefined

IMUL Operands	Clocks	Transfers	Bytes	IMUL Coding Example
immed8*	(22-25)	-	3	IMUL 6
immed16*	(29-32)	-	4	IMUL 20
reg8	80-98(25-28)	-	2	IMUL CL
reg16	128-154			
	(34-37)	-	2	IMUL BX
mem8	86-104			
	+EA(31-34)	1	2-4	IMUL RATE_BYTE
mem16	134-160			
	+EA(40-43)	1	2-4	IMUL RATE_WORD[BP][DI]

IN   INPUT BYTE OR WORD   IN

Operation:

(DEST) ← (SRC)

Flags Affected:

None

IN Operands	Clocks	Transfers	Bytes	IN Coding Example
accumulator, immed8	10(10)	1	2	IN AL, OEAH
accumulator,DX	8(8)	1	1	IN AX, DX

INC   INCREMENT   INC

Operation:

(DEST) ← (DEST) + 1

Flags Affected:

AF, OF, PF, SF, ZF

INC Operands	Clocks	Transfers	Bytes	INC Coding Example
reg16	3(3)	-	1	INC CX
reg8	3(3)	-	2	INC BL
memory	15(15)+EA	2	2-4	INC ALPHA [DI][BX]

INS   INPUT STRING   INS

Operation:

(DEST) ← (SRC)

Flags Affected:

None

INS Operands	Clocks	Transfers	Bytes	INS Coding Example
dest-string,port*	(14)	2	1	INS BUFF1, USART D
(repeat)dest-string, port*	(8+8/rep)	2/rep	1	REP INS BUFF1, USART D

INT   INTERRUPT   INT

Operation:

(SP) ← (SP) - 2
((SP) + 1:(SP)) ← FLAGS
(IF) ← 0
(TF) ← 0
(SP) ← (SP) - 2
((SP) + 1:(SP)) ← (CS)
(CS) ← (TYPE * 4 + 2)
(SP) ← (SP) - 2
((SP) + 1:(SP)) ← (IP)
(IP) ← (TYPE * 4)

Flags Affected:

IF, TF

INT Operands	Clocks	Transfers	Bytes	INT Coding Example
immed8(type=3)	52(45)	5	1	INT 3
immed8(type≠3)	51(47)	5	2	INT 67

INTO   INTERRUPT ON OVERFLOW   INTO

Operation:

if (OF) = 1 then
  (SP) ← (SP) - 2
  ((SP) + 1:(SP)) ← FLAGS
  (IF) ← 0
  (TF) ← 0
  (SP) ← (SP) - 2
  ((SP) + 1:(SP)) ← (CS)
  (CS) ← (12H)
  (SP) ← (SP) - 2
  ((SP) + 1:(SP)) ← (IP)
  (IP) ← (10H)

Flags Affected:

None

INTO Operands	Clocks	Transfers	Bytes	INTO Coding Example
(no operands)	53 or 4 (48 or 4)	5	1	INTO

IRET   INTERRUPT RETURN   IRET

Operation:

(IP) ← ((SP) + 1:(SP))
(SP) ← (SP) + 2
(CS) ← ((SP) + 1:(SP))
(SP) ← (SP) + 2
FLAGS ← ((SP) + 1:(SP))
(SP) ← (SP) + 2

Flags Affected:

All

IRET Operands	Clocks	Transfers	Bytes	IRET Coding Example
(no operands)	32(28)	3	1	IRET

JA   JUMP ON ABOVE   JA

JNBE   JUMP ON NOT BELOW OR EQUAL   JNBE

Operation:

if (CF) & (ZF) = 0 then
  (IP) ← (IP) + disp (sign-extended
    to 16-bits)

Flags Affected:

None

JA/JNBE Operands	Clocks	Transfers	Bytes	JA Coding Example
short-label	16 or 4 (13 or 4)	-	2	JA ABOVE
				JNBE Coding Example
				JNBE ABOVE

JAE

JUMP ON ABOVE OR EQUAL

JAE

JNB

JUMP ON NOT BELOW

JNB

Operation: **Flags Affected:**

if (CF) = 0 then   None
  (IP) ← (IP) + disp (sign-extended
    to 16-bits)

JAE/JNB Operands	Clocks	Transfers	Bytes	JAE Coding Example
short-label	16 or 4 (13 or 4)	-	2	JAE ABOVE_EQUAL

JB

JUMP ON BELOW

JB

JNAE

JUMP ON NOT ABOVE OR EQUAL

JNAE

Operation: **Flags Affected:**

if (CF) = 1 then   None
  (IP) ← (IP) + disp (sign-extended
    to 16-bits)

JB/JNAE Operands	Clocks	Transfers	Bytes	JB Coding Example
short-label	16 or 4 (13 or 4)	-	2	JB BELOW

JBE

JUMP ON BELOW OR EQUAL

JBE

JNA

JUMP ON NOT ABOVE

JNA

Operation: **Flags Affected:**

IF (CF) or (ZF) = 1 then   None
  (IP) ← (IP) + disp (sign-extended
    to 16-bits)

JBE/JNA Operands	Clocks	Transfers	Bytes	JNA Coding Example
short-label	16 or 4 (13 or 4)	-	2	JNA NOT_ABOVE

JC   JUMP ON CARRY   JC

Operation: Flags Affected:

if (CF) = 1 then   None
  (IP) ← (IP) + disp (sign-extended
    to 16-bits)

JC Operands	Clocks	Transfers	Bytes	JC Coding Example
short-label	16 or 4 (13 or 4)	-	2	JC CARRY_SET

JCXZ   JUMP IF CX REGISTER ZERO   JCXZ

Operation: Flags Affected:

if (CX) = 0 then   None
  (IP) ← (IP) + disp (sign-extended
    to 16-bits)

JCXZ Operands	Clocks	Transfers	Bytes	JCXZ Coding Example
short-label	18 or 6 (16 or 5)	-	2	JCXZ COUNT_DONE

JE   JUMP ON EQUAL   JE
JZ   JUMP ON ZERO   JZ

Operation: Flags Affected:

if (ZF) = 1 then   None
  (IP) ← (IP) + disp (sign-extended
    to 16-bits)

JE/JZ Operands	Clocks	Transfers	Bytes	JZ Coding Example
short-label	16 or 4 (13 or 4)	-	2	JZ ZERO

JG
JNLE

JUMP ON GREATER
JUMP ON NOT LESS OR EQUAL

JG
JNLE

Operation:

if ((SF) = (OF)) or (ZF) = 0 then
   (IP) ← (IP) + disp (sign-extended
      to 16-bits)

Flags Affected:

None

JG/JNLE Operands	Clocks	Transfers	Bytes	JG Coding Example
short-label	16 or 4 (13 or 4)	-	2	JG GREATER

JGE

JUMP ON GREATER OR EQUAL

JGE

JNL

JUMP ON NOT LESS

JNL

Operation:

if (SF) = (OF) then
   (IP) ← (IP) + disp (sign-extended
      to 16-bits)

Flags Affected:

None

JGE/JNL Operands	Clocks	Transfers	Bytes	JGE Coding Example
short-label	16 or 4 (13 or 4)	-	2	JGE GREATER_EQUAL

JL

JUMP ON LESS

JL

JNGE

JUMP ON NOT GREATER OR EQUAL

JNGE

Operation:

if (SF) ≠ (OF) then
   (IP) ← (IP) + disp (sign-extended
      to 16-bits)

Flags Affected:

None

JL/JNGE Operands	Clocks	Transfers	Bytes	JL Coding Example
short-label	16 or 4 (13 or 4)	-	2	JL LESS

JLE   JUMP ON LESS OR EQUAL   JLE

JNG   JUMP ON NOT GREATER   JNG

Operation:

if ((SF) ≠ (OF)) or ((ZF) = 1) then
(IP) ← (IP) + disp (sign-extended
to 16-bits)

Flags Affected:

None

JLE/JNG Operands	Clocks	Transfers	Bytes	JNG Coding Example
short-label	16 or 4 (13 or 4)	-	2	JNG NOT_GREATER

JMP   JUMP UNCONDITIONALLY   JMP

Operation:

if Inter-Segment then (CS) ← SEG
(IP) ← DEST

Flags Affected:

None

JMP Operands	Clocks	Transfers	Bytes	JMP Coding Example
short-label	15(13)	-	2	JMP SHORT
near-label	15(13)	-	3	JMP WITHIN_SEGMENT
far-label	15(13)	-	5	JMP FAR_LABEL
memptr16	18(17)+EA	-	2-4	JMP[BX].TARGET
regptr16	11(11)	-	2	JMP CX
memptr32	24(26)+EA	-	2-4	JMP OTHER.SEG[SI]

JNC   JUMP ON NOT CARRY   JNC

Operation:

if (CF) = 0 THEN
(IP) ← (IP) + disp (sign-extended
to 16-bits)

Flags Affected:

None

JNC Operands	Clocks	Transfers	Bytes	JNC Coding Example
short-label	16 or 4 (13 or 4)	-	2	JNC NO_CARRY

JNE   JUMP ON NOT EQUAL   JNE
JNZ   JUMP ON NOT ZERO   JNZ

Operation: **Flags Affected:**

if (ZF) = 0 then   None
  (IP) ← (IP) + disp (sign-extended
    to 16-bits)

JNE/JNZ Operands	Clocks	Transfers	Bytes	JNE Coding Example
short-label	16 or 4 (13 or 4)	-	2	JNE NOT_EQUAL

JNO   JUMP ON NOT OVERFLOW   JNO

Operation: **Flags Affected:**

if (OF) = 0 then   None
  (IP) ← (IP) + disp (sign-extended
    to 16-bits)

JNO Operands	Clocks	Transfers	Bytes	JNO Coding Example
short-label	16 or 4 (13 or 4)	-	2	JNO NO_OVERFLOW

JNS   JUMP ON NOT SIGN   JNS

Operation: **Flags Affected:**

if (SF) = 0 then   None
  (IP) ← (IP) + disp (sign-extended
    to 16-bits)

JNS Operands	Clocks	Transfers	Bytes	JNS Coding Example
short-label	16 or 4 (13 or 4)	-	2	JNS POSITIVE

JNP   JUMP ON NOT PARITY   JNP

JPO   JUMP ON PARITY ODD   JPO

Operation:

if (PF) = 0 then
  (IP) ← (IP) + disp (sign-extended
    to 16-bits)

Flags Affected:

None

JNP/JPO Operands	Clocks	Transfers	Bytes	JPO Coding Example
short-label	16 or 4 (13 or 4)	-	2	JPO ODD_PARITY

JO   JUMP ON OVERFLOW   JO

Operation:

if (OF) = 1 then
  (IP) ← (IP) + disp (sign-extended
    to 16-bits)

Flags Affected:

None

JO Operands	Clocks	Transfers	Bytes	JO Coding Example
short-label	16 or 4 (13 or 4)	-	2	JO SIGNED_OVERFLOW

JP   JUMP ON PARITY   JP

JPE   JUMP ON PARITY EQUAL   JPE

Operation:

if (PF) = 1 then
  (IP) ← (IP) + disp (sign-extended
    to 16-bits)

Flags Affected:

None

JP/JPE Operands	Clocks	Transfers	Bytes	JPE Coding Example
short-label	16 or 4 (13 or 4)	-	2	JPE EVEN_PARITY

JS   JUMP ON SIGN   JS

Operation: **Flags Affected:**

if (SF) = 1 then   None
  (IP) ← (IP) + disp (sign-extended
    to 16-bits)

JS Operands	Clocks	Transfers	Bytes	JS Coding Example
short-label	16 or 4 (13 or 4)	-	2	JS NEGATIVE

LAHF   LOAD REGISTER AH   LAHF
FROM FLAGS

Operation: **Flags Affected:**

(AH) ← (SF):(ZF):X:(AF):X:(PF):X:(CF)   None

LAHF Operands	Clocks	Transfers	Bytes	LAHF Coding Example
(no operands)	4(2)	-	1	LAHF

LDS   LOAD POINTER USING DS   LDS

Operation: **Flags Affected:**

(REG) ← (EA)   None
(DS) ← (EA + 2)

LDS Operands	Clocks	Transfers	Bytes	LDS Coding Example
reg16, mem32	16(18) + EA	2	2-4	LDS SI, DATA.SEG[DI]

LEA   LOAD EFFECTIVE   LEA
ADDRESS

Operation: **Flags Affected:**

(REG) ← EA   None

LEA Operands	Clocks	Transfers	Bytes	LEA Coding Example
reg16, mem16	2(6) + EA	-	2-4	LEA BX,[BP][DI]

LEAVE   RESTORE STACK   LEAVE
FOR PROCEDURE EXIT

Operation:

Flags Affected:

None

(SP) ← (BP)
(BP) ← ((SP) + 1 : (SP))
(SP) ← (SP) + 2

LEAVE Operands	Clocks	Transfers	Bytes	LEAVE Coding Example
(no operands)*	8	1	1	LEAVE

LES   LOAD POINTER USING ES   LES

Operation:

Flags Affected:

(REG) ← (EA)
(ES) ← (EA + 2)

None

LES Operands	Clocks	Transfers	Bytes	LES Coding Example
reg16, mem32	16(18)+EA	2	2-4	LES DI,[BX].TEXT_BUFF

LOCK   LOCK THE BUS   LOCK

Operation:

Flags Affected:

None

None

LOCK Operands	Clocks	Transfers	Bytes	LOCK Coding Example
(no operands)	2(2)	-	1	LOCK XCHG FLAG, AL

LODS   LOAD STRING (BYTE OR WORD)   LODS

Operation: **Flags Affected:**

(DEST) ← (SRC)   None
if (DF) = 0 then (SI) ← (SI) + DELTA
else (SI) ← (SI) - DELTA

LODS Operands	Clocks	Transfers	Bytes	LODS Coding Example
source-string	12(10)	1	1	LODS CUSTOMER_NAME
(repeat)	9+13			
source-string	(6+11/rep)	1/rep	1	REP LODS NAME

LOOP   LOOP   LOOP

Operation: **Flags Affected:**

(CX) ← (CX) - 1   None
if (CX) ≠ 0 then
   (IP) ← (IP) + disp (sign-extended
      to 16-bits)

LOOP Operands	Clocks	Transfers	Bytes	LOOP Coding Example
short-label	17 or 5	-	2	LOOP AGAIN
	(15 or 5)			

LOOPE   LOOP WHILE EQUAL   LOOPE

LOOPZ   LOOP WHILE ZERO   LOOPZ

Operation: **Flags Affected:**

(CX) ← (CX) - 1   None
if (ZF) = 1 and (CX) ≠ 0 then
   (IP) ← (IP) + disp (sign-extended
      to 16-bits)

LOOPE/LOOPZ Operands	Clocks	Transfers	Bytes	LOOPE Coding Example
short-label	18 or 6	-	2	LOOPE AGAIN
	(16 or 6)			

LOOPNZ LOOP WHILE NOT ZERO LOOPNZ

LOOPNE LOOP WHILE NOT EQUAL LOOPNE

Operation:

(CX) ← (CX) - 1
if (ZF) = 0 and (CX) ≠ 0 then
 (IP) ← (IP) + disp (sign-extended
  to 16-bits)

Flags Affected:

None

LOOPNE/LOOPNZ Operands	Clocks	Transfers	Bytes	LOOPNE Coding Example
short-label	19 or 5 (16 or 5)	-	2	LOOPNE AGAIN

MOV MOVE (BYTE OR WORD) MOV

Operation:

(DEST) ← (SRC)

Flags Affected:

None

MOV Operands	Clocks	Transfers	Bytes	MOV Coding Example
memory, accumulator	10(9)	1	3	MOV ARRAY AL
accumulator, memory	10(8)	1	3	MOV AX,TEMP_RESULT
register, register	2(2)	-	2	MOV AX, CX
register, memory	8(12)+EA	1	2-4	MOV BP, STACK_TOP
memory, register	9(9)+EA	1	2-4	MOV COUNT [DI],CX
register, immediate	4(3-4)	-	2-3	MOV CL,2
memory, immediate	10(12-13) + EA	1	3-6	MOV MASK[BX][SI],2CH
seg-reg, reg16	2(2)	-	2	MOV ES, CX
seg-reg, mem16	8(9)+EA	1	2-4	MOV DS,SEGMENT_BASE
reg16, seg-reg	2(2)	-	2	MOV BP, SS
memory, seg-reg	9(11)+EA	1	2-4	MOV[BX],SEG_SAVE,CS

MOVS   MOVE STRING   MOVS

Operation:

(DEST) ← (SRC)

Flags Affected:

None

MOVS Operands	Clocks	Transfers	Bytes	MOVS Coding Example

dest-string,
  source-string
(repeat) dest-string,
  source-string
	18(9)
	9+17/rep
	(8+8/rep)
		2
		
		2/rep
			1
			
			1
				MOVS LINE EDIT DATA
				
				REP MOVS SCREEN,
				  BUFFER

MUL   MULTIPLY   MUL

Operation:

(DES) ← (LSRC) * (RSRC), where *
  is unsigned multiply
if (EXT) = 0 then (CF) ← 0
else (CF) ← 1;
(OF) ← (CF)

Flags Affected:

CF, OF.
AF, PF, SF, ZF undefined

MUL Operands	Clocks	Transfers	Bytes	MUL Coding Example
reg8	70-77 (26-28)	-	2	MUL BL
reg16	118-113 (35-37)	-	2	MUL CX
mem8	76-83 + EA(32-34)	1	2-4	MUL MONTH [SI]
mem16	124-139 +EA(41-43)	1	2-4	MUL BAUD_RATE

NEG   NEGATE   NEG

Operation:

(EA) ← SRC - (EA)
(EA) ← (EA) + 1 (affecting flags)

Flags Affected:

AF, CF, OF, PF, SF, ZF

NEG Operands	Clocks	Transfers	Bytes	NEG Coding Example
register memory	3(3) 16(3)+EA	- 2	2 2-4	NEG AL NEG MULTIPLIER

NOP   NO OPERATION   NOP

Operation:

None

Flags Affected:

None

NOP Operands	Clocks	Transfers	Bytes	NOP Coding Example
(no operands)	3(3)	-	1	NOP

NOT   LOGICAL NOT   NOT

Operation:

$(EA) \leftarrow SRC - (EA)$

Flags Affected:

None

NOT Operands	Clocks	Transfers	Bytes	NOT Coding Example
register	3(3)	-	-	NOT AX
memory	16(3)+EA	2	-	NOT CHARACTER

OR   LOGICAL OR   OR

Operation:

$(DEST) \leftarrow (LSRC)$ OR $(RSRC)$
$(CF) \leftarrow 0$
$(OF) \leftarrow 0$

Flags Affected:

CF, OF, PF, SF, ZF.
AF undefined

OR Operands	Clocks	Transfers	Bytes	OR Coding Example
register,register	3(3)	-	2	OR AL, BL
register, memory	9(10)+EA	1	2-4	OR DX,PORT_ID[DI]
memory,register	16(10)+EA	2	2-4	OR FLAG_BYTE, CL
accumulator, immediate	4(3-4)	-	2-3	OR AL, 01101100B
register, immediate	4(4)	-	3-4	OR CX, 01H
memory, immediate	17(16)+EA	2	3-6	OR[BX].CMD_WORD,0CFH

OUT   OUTPUT   OUT

Operation: Flags Affected:

(DEST) ← (SRC)   None

OUT Operands	Clocks*	Transfers	Bytes	OUT Coding Example
immed8,accumulator	10(9)	1	2	OUT 44, AX
DX, accumulator	8(7)	1	1	OUT DX, AL

OUTS   OUTPUT STRING   OUTS

Operation: Flags Affected:

                                        None

(DST) ← (SRC)

OUTS Operands	Clocks	Transfers	Bytes	OUTS Coding Example
port,source-string*	(14)	2	1	OUTS PORT2, BUFF2
(repeat) port, source-string*	(8+8/rep)	2/rep	1	REP OUTS PORT4, BUFF2

POP   POP   POP

Operation: Flags Affected:

(DEST) ← ((SP)+1:(SP))   None
(SP) ← (SP)+2

POP Operands	Clocks	Transfers	Bytes	POP Coding Example
register	8(10)	1	1	POP DX
seg-reg(CS illegal)	8(8)	1	1	POP DS
memory	17(20)+EA	2	2-4	POP PARAMETER

POPA   POP ALL REGISTERS   POPA

Operation:

Flags Affected:

None

(DI) ← ((SP) + 1: (SP))
(SP) ← (SP) + 2
(SI) ←
(SP) ← (SP) + 2
(BP) ← ((SP) + 1: (SP))
(SP) ← (SP) + 2
(BX) ← ((SP) + 1: (SP))
(SP) ← (SP) + 2
(DX) ← ((SP) + 1: (SP))
(SP) ← (SP) + 2
(CX) ← ((SP) + 1: (SP))
(SP) ← (SP) + 2
(AX) ← ((SP + 1: (SP))
(SP) ← (SP) + 2

POPA Operands	Clocks	Transfers	Bytes	POPA Coding Example
(no operands)*	(51)	8	1	POPA

POPF   POP FLAGS   POPF

Operation:

Flags Affected:

Flags ← ((SP) + 1:(SP))
(SP) ← (SP) + 2

All

POPF Operands	Clocks	Transfers	Bytes	POPF Coding Example
(no operands)	8(8)	1	1	POPF

PUSH   PUSH   PUSH

Operation:

$(SP) \leftarrow (SP) - 2$
$((SP) + 1:(SP)) \leftarrow (SRC)$

Flags Affected:

None

PUSH Operands	Clocks	Transfers	Bytes	PUSH Coding Example
register	11(10)	1	1	PUSH SI
seg-reg(CS legal)	10(9)	1	1	PUSH ES
memory	16(16)+EA	2	2-4	PUSH RETURN_CODE[SI]

PUSHA   PUSH ALL REGISTERS   PUSHA

Operation:

$temp \leftarrow (SP)$
$(SP) \leftarrow (SP) - 2$
$((SP) + 1: (SP)) \leftarrow (AX)$
$(SP) \leftarrow (SP) - 2$
$((SP) + 1: (SP)) \leftarrow (CX)$
$(SP) \leftarrow (SP) - 2$
$((SP) + 1: (SP)) \leftarrow (DX)$
$(SP) \leftarrow (SP) - 2$
$((SP) + 1: (SP)) \leftarrow (BX)$
$(SP) \leftarrow (SP) - 2$
$((SP) + 1: (SP)) \leftarrow (SP)$
$(SP) \leftarrow (SP) - 2$
$((SP) + 1: (SP)) \leftarrow (SP)$
$(SP) \leftarrow (SP) - 2$
$((SP) + 1: (SP)) \leftarrow (BP)$
$(SP) \leftarrow (SP) - 2$
$((SP) + 1: (SP)) \leftarrow (SI)$
$(SP) \leftarrow (SP) - 2$
$((SP) + 1: (SP)) \leftarrow (DI)$

Flags Affected:

None

PUSHA Operands	Clocks	Transfers	Bytes	PUSHA Coding Example
(no operands)*	(36)	8	1	PUSHA

PUSHF   PUSH FLAGS   PUSHF

Operation:

(SP) ← (SP) - 2
((SP) + 1:(SP)) ← Flags

Flags Affected:

None

PUSHF Operands	Clocks	Transfers	Bytes	PUSHF Coding Example
(no operands)	10(9)	1	1	PUSHF

RCL   ROTATE THROUGH CARRY LEFT   RCL

Operation:

(temp) ← COUNT
do while (temp) ≠ 0
   (tmpcf) ← (CF)
   (CF) ← high-order bit of (EA)
   (EA) ← (EA) * 2 + (tmpcf)
   (temp) ← (temp) - 1
if COUNT = 1 then
   if high-order bit of (EA) ≠ (CF)
      then (OF) ← 1
   else (OF) ← 0
else (OF) undefined

Flags Affected:

CF, OF

RCL Operands	Clocks	Transfers	Bytes	RCL Coding Example
register, n*	(5 + 1/bit)	-	3	RCL CX, 5
memory, n*	(17 + 1/bit)	2	3-5	RCL ALPHA, 5
register 1,	2(2)	-	2	RCL CX, 1
register, CL	8 + 4/bit			
	(5 + 1/bit)	-	2	RCL AL, CL
memory, 1	15(15) + EA	2	2-4	RCL ALPHA, 1
memory, CL	20 + 4/bit			
	(17 + 1/bit) + EA	2	2-4	RCL[BP].PARAM, CL

RCR

ROTATE THROUGH CARRY RIGHT

RCR

Operation:

(temp) ← COUNT
do while (temp) ≠ 0
  (tmpcf) ← (CF)
  (CF) ← low-order bit of (EA)
  (EA) ← (EA) / 2
  high-order bit of (EA) ← (tmpcf)
  (temp) ← (temp) - 1
if COUNT = 1 then
  if high-order bit of (EA) ≠ next-
      to-high-order bit of (EA)
    then (OF) ← 1
  else (OF) ← 0
else (OF) undefined

Flags Affected:

CF, OF

RCR Operands	Clocks	Transfers	Bytes	RCR Coding Example
register, n*	(5 + 1/bit)	-	3	RCR BX, 5
memory, n*	(17 + 1/bit)	2	3-5	RCR [BX].STATUS, 5
register, 1	2(2)	-	2	RCR BX, 1
register, CL	8 + 4/bit			
	(5 + 1/bit)	-	2	RCR BL, CL
memory, 1	15(15) + EA	2	2-4	RCR [BX].STATUS, 1
memory, CL	20 + 4/bit			
	(17 + 1/bit) + EA	2	2-4	RCR ARRAY[DI], CL

REP   REPEAT   REP

REPE/REPZ   REPE/REPZ
REPEAT WHILE EQUAL/
REPEAT WHILE ZERO

REPNE/REPNZ REPNE/REPNZ
REPEAT WHILE NOT EQUAL/
REPEAT WHILE NOT ZERO

Operation:

do while (CX) ≠ 0
  service pending interrupt (if
  any) execute primitive string
    operation in succeeding byte
  (CX) ← (CX) - 1
  if primitive operation is CMPB,
  CMPW, SCAB, or SCAW and
  (ZF) ≠ z then exit from
  while loop

Flags Affected:

None

REP Operands	Clocks	Transfers	Bytes	REP Coding Example
(no operands)	2(2)	—	1	REP MOVS DEST, SRCE
REPE/REPZ Operands	Clocks	Transfers	Bytes	REPE Coding Example
(no operands)	2(2)	—	1	REPE CMPS DATA, KEY
REPNE/REPNZ Operands	Clocks	Transfers	Bytes	REPNE Coding Example
(no operands)	2(2)	—	1	REPNE SCAS INPUT LINE

RET   RETURN   RET

Operation:

(IP) ← ((SP)=1:(SP))
(SP) ← (SP) + 2
if Inter-Segment then
  (CS) ← ((SP) + 1:(SP))
  (SP) ← (SP) + 2
if Add Immediate to Stack Pointer
  then (SP) ← (SP) + data

Flags Affected:

None

RET Operands	Clocks	Transfers	Bytes	RET Coding Example
(intra-segment, no pop)	16(16)	1	1	RET
(intra-segment,pop)	20(18)	1	3	RET 4
(inter-segment, no pop)	26(22)	2	1	RET
(inter-segment,pop)	25(25)	2	3	RET 2

ROL   ROTATE LEFT   ROL

Operation:

(temp) ← COUNT
do while (temp) ≠ 0
  (CF) ← high-order bit of (EA)
  (EA) ← (EA) * 2 + (CF)
  (temp) ← (temp) - 1
if COUNT = 1 then
  if high-order bit of (EA) ≠ (CF)
    then (OF) ← 1
  else (OF) ← 0
else (OF) undefined

Flags Affected:

CF, OF

ROL Operands	Clocks	Transfers	Bytes	ROL Coding Example
register, n*	(5 + 1/bit)	-	3	ROL BX,5
memory, n*	(17 + 1/bit)	2	3-5	ROL FLAG_BYTE[DI],5
register, 1	2(2)	-	2	ROL BX, 1
register, CL	8 + 4/bit			
	(5 + 1/bit)	-	2	ROL DI, CL
memory, 1	15(15) + EA	2	2-4	ROL FLAG_BYTE[DI],1
memory, CL	20 + 4/bit			
	(17 + 1/bit) + EA	2	2-4	ROL ALPHA, CL

ROR   ROTATE RIGHT   ROR

Operation:

(temp) ← COUNT
do while (temp) ≠ 0
  (CF) ← low-order bit of (EA)
  (EA) ← (EA) / 2
  high-order bit of (EA) ← (CF)
  (temp) ← (temp) - 1
if COUNT = 1 then
  if high-order bit of (EA) ≠ next-
to-high-order bit of (EA)
then (OF) ← 1
  else (OF) ← 0
else (OF) undefined

Flags Affected:

CF, OF

ROR Operands	Clocks	Transfers	Bytes	ROR Coding Example
register, n*	(5 + 1/bit)	-	3	ROR AL, 5
memory, n*	(17 + 1/bit)	2	3-5	ROR PORT_STATUS, 5
register, 1	2(2)	-	2	ROR AL, 1
register, Cl	8 + 4/bit			
	(5 + 1/bit)	-	2	ROR BX, CL
memory, 1	15(15) + EA	2	2-4	ROR PORT_STATUS, 1
memory, CL	20 + 4/bit			
	(17 + 1/bit) + EA	2	2-4	ROR CMD_WORD, CL

SAHF   STORE REGISTER AH   SAHF
INTO FLAGS

Operation:

(SF):(ZF):X:(AF):X:(PF):X:(CF) ← (AH)

Flags Affected:

AF, CF, PF, SF, ZF

SAHF Operands	Clocks	Transfers	Bytes	SAHF Coding Example
(no operands)	4(3)	-	1	SAHF

SAL   SHIFT ARITHMETIC LEFT   SAL
SHL   SHIFT LOGICAL LEFT   SHL

Operation:

```
(temp) ← COUNT
do while (temp) ≠ 0
  (CF) ← high-order bit of (EA)
  (EA) ← (EA) * 2
  (temp) ← (temp) - 1
if COUNT = 1 then
  if high-order bit of (EA) ≠ (CE)
    then (OF) ← 1
  else (OF) ← 0
else (OF) undefined
```

Flags Affected:

CF, OF, PF, SF, ZF.
AF undefined

SAL/SHL Operands	Clocks	Transfers	Bytes	SAL/SHL Coding Example
register, n*	(5 + 1/bit)	-	3	SAL AH, 5
memory, n*	(17 + 1/bit)	2	3-5	SAL[BX].OVERDRAW, 5
register, 1	2(2)	-	2	SAL AH, 1
register, CL	8 + 4/bit			
	(5 + 1/bit)	-	2	SHL DI, CL
memory, 1	15(15) + EA	2	2-4	SHL[BX].OVERDRAW, 1
memory, CL	20 + 4/bit			
	(17 + 1/bit) + EA	2	2-4	SAL STORE_COUNT, CL

SAR SHIFT ARITHMETIC RIGHT SAR

Operation:

(temp) ← COUNT
do while (temp) ≠ 0
  (CF) ← low-order bit of (EA)
  (EA) ← (EA) / 2, where / is
    equivalent to signed division,
    rounding down
  (temp) ← (temp) - 1
if COUNT = 1 then
  if high-order bit of (EA) ≠ next-
    to-high-order bit of (EA)
    then (OF) ← 1
  else (OF) ← 0
else (OF) ← 0

Flags Affected:

CF, OF, PF, SF, ZF.
AF undefined

SAR Operands	Clocks	Transfers	Bytes	SAR Coding Example
register, n*	(5 + 1/bit)	-	3	SAR DX, 5
memory, n*	(17 + 1/bit)	2	3-5	SAR N_BLOCKS, 5
register, 1	2(2)	-	2	SAR DX, 1
register, CL	8 + 4/bit			
	(5 + 1/bit)	-	2	SAR DI, CL
memory, 1	15(15) + EA	2	2-4	SAR N_BLOCKS, 1
memory, CL	20 + 4/bit			
	(17 + 1/bit) + EA	2	2-4	SAR N_BLOCKS, CL

SBB SUBTRACT WITH BORROW SBB

Operation:

if (CF) = 1 then (DEST) = (LSRC) -
  (RSRC) - 1
else (DEST) ← (LSRC) - (RSRC)

Flags Affected:

AF, CF, OF, PF, SF, ZF

SBB Operands	Clocks	Transfers	Bytes	SBB Coding Example
register, register	3(3)	-	2	SBB BX, CX
register, memory	9(10) + EA	1	2-4	SBB DI,[BX].PAYMENT
memory, register	16(10) + EA	2	2-4	SBB BALANCE, AX
accumulator, immediate	4(3-4)	-	2-3	SBB AX, 2
register, immediate	4(4)	-	3-4	SBB CL, 1
memory, immediate	17(16) + EA	2	3 6	SBB COUNT [SI], 10

SCAS   SCAN (BYTE OR WORD) STRING   SCAS

Operation:

(LSRC) - RSRC)
if (DF) = 0 then (DI) ← (DI) + DELTA
else (DI) ← (DI) - DELTA

Flags Affected:

AF, CF, OF, PF, SF, ZF

SCAS Operands	Clocks	Transfers	Bytes	SCAS Coding Example
dest-string	15(15)	1	1	SCAS INPUT_LINE
(repeat)dest-string	9+15			
	(5+15/rep)	1/rep	1	REPNE SCAS BUFFER

SHR   SHIFT LOGICAL RIGHT   SHR

Operation:

(temp) ← COUNT
do while (temp) ≠ 0
  CF) ← low-order bit of (EA
  (EA) ← (EA) / 2, where / is
     equivalent to unsigned
     division
  (temp) ← (temp) - 1
if COUNT = 1 then
  if high-order bit of (EA) ≠ next-
    to-high-order bit of (EA)
    then (OF) ← 1
  else (OF) ← 0
else (OF) undefined

Flags Affected:

CF, OF, PF, SF, ZF.
AF undefined

SHR Operands	Clocks	Transfers	Bytes	SHR Coding Example
register, n*	(5+1/bit)	-	3	SHR SI, 5
memory, n*	(17+1/bit)	2	3-5	SHR ID_BYTE[SI][BX], 5
register, 1	2(2)	-	2	SHR SI, 1
register, CL	8+4/bit			
	(5+1/bit)	-	2	SHR SI, CL
memory, 1	15(15)+EA	2	2-4	SHR ID_BYTE[SI][BX], 1
memory, CL	20+4/bit			
	(17+1/bit)+EA	2	2-4	SHR INPUT_WORD, CL

STC   SET CARRY   STC

Operation: **Flags Affected:**

(CF) ← 1   CF

STC Operands	Clocks	Transfers	Bytes	STC Coding Example
(no operands)	2(2)	-	1	STC

STD   SET DIRECTION FLAG   STD

Operation: **Flags Affected:**

(DF) ← 1   DF

STD Operands	Clocks	Transfers	Bytes	STD Coding Example
(no operands)	2(2)	-	1	STD

STI   SET INTERRUPT-   STI
ENABLE FLAG

Operation: **Flags Affected:**

(IF) ← 1   IF

STI Operands	Clocks	Transfers	Bytes	STI Coding Example
(no operands)	2(2)	-	1	STI

STOS   STORE (BYTE/OR/   STOS
WORD) STRING

Operation: **Flags Affected:**

(DEST) ← (SRC)   None
if (DF) = 0 then (DI) ← (DI) + DELTA
else (DI) ← (DI) - DELTA

STOS Operands	Clocks	Transfers	Bytes	STOS Coding Example
dest-string	11(10)	1	1	STOP PRINT_LINE
(repeat)dest-string	9+10/rep (6+9/rep)	1/rep	1	REP STOS DISPLAY

SUB   SUBTRACT   SUB

Operation:

(DEST) ← (LSRC) - (RSRC)

Flags Affected:

AF, CF, OF, PF, SF, ZF

SUB Operands	Clocks	Transfers	Bytes	SUB Coding Example
register, register	3(3)	-	2	SUB CX, BX
register, memory	9(10)+EA	1	2-4	SUB DX,MATH_TOTAL[SI]
memory, register	16(10)+EA	2	2-4	SUB[BP + 2], C̄L
accumulator, immediate	4(3-4)	-	2-3	SUB AL, 10
register, immediate	4(4)	-	3-4	SUB SI, 5280
memory, immediate	17(16)+EA	2	3-6	SUB[BP].BALANCE, 1000

TEST   TEST   TEST

Operation:

(LSRC) & (RSRC)
(CF) ← 0
(OF) ← 0

Flags Affected:

CF, OF, PF, SF, ZF.
AF undefined

TEST Operands	Clocks	Transfers	Bytes	TEST Coding Example
register, register	3(3)	-	2	TEST SI, DI
register, memory	9(10)+EA	1	2-4	TEST SI, END_COUNT
accumulator, immediate	4(3-4)	-	2-3	TEST AL, 00100000B
register, immediate	5(4)	-	3-4	TEST BX, 0CC4H
memory, immediate	11(10)+EA	-	3-6	TEST RETURN_CODE,01H

WAIT   WAIT   WAIT

Operation:

None

Flags Affected:

None

WAIT Operands	Clocks	Transfers	Bytes	WAIT Coding Example
(no operands)	4+5n(6)	-	1	WAIT

XCHG   EXCHANGE   XCHG

Operation:

(temp) ← (DEST)
(DEST) ← (SRC)
(SRC) ← (temp)

Flags Affected:

None

XCHG Operands	Clocks	Transfers	Bytes	XCHG Coding Example
accumulator,reg16	3(3)	-	1	XCHG AX, BX
memory, register	17(17)+EA	2	2-4	XCHG SEMAPHORE, AX
register, register	4(4)	-	2	XCHG AL, BL

XLAT   TRANSLATE   XLAT

Operation:

AL ← ((BX) + (AL))

Flags Affected:

None

XLAT Operands	Clocks	Transfers	Bytes	XLAT Coding Example
source-table	11(11)	1	1	XLAT ASCII_TAB

XOR   EXCLUSIVE OR   XOR

Operation:

(DEST) ← (LSRC) XOR (RSRC)
(CF) ← 0
(OF) ← 0

Flags Affected:

CF, OF, PF, SF, ZF.
AF undefined

XOR Operands	Clocks	Transfers	Bytes	XOR Coding Example
register, register	3(3)	-	2	XOR CX, BX
register, memory	9(10)+EA	1	2-4	XOR CL, MASK_BYTE
memory, register	16(10)+EA	2	2-4	XOR ALPHA[SI],DX
accumulator, immediate	4(3-4)	-	2-3	XOR AL, 01000010B
register, immediate	4(4)	-	3-4	XOR SI, 00C2H
memory, immediate	17(16)+EA	2	3-6	XOR RETURN_CODE,0D2H

INDEX

About the Author

Dr. Skinner has over twenty years of experience in the computer field. On the faculty of Boston University since 1979, he is currently an Assistant Professor of Computer Science. One of his past affiliations was M.I.T. Project MAC, where he worked on the Multics operating system and the ARPA computer network. He has done extensive consulting on microprocessor hardware and software systems, and has programmed a wide variety of computers, from mainframes to most of the current 8- and 16-bit micropro- cessors. His collection of computers at home includes a Digital Equipment Corporation Rainbow, which uses the 8088 chip, a DEC LSI/11, and a Data General/One, which also uses the 8088.